Beyond Disney

the
Unofficial
Guide® to
Universal,
SeaWorld, and the
Best of Central
Florida

Also available from Macmillan Travel:

Beyond Disney

the Unofficial Guide® to

Universal,
SeaWorld, and the
Best of Central
Florida

Bob Sehlinger
and Amber Morris

Macmillan • USA

Macmillan Travel
Macmillan General Reference USA, Inc.
1633 Broadway
New York, New York 10019-6785

Produced by Menasha Ridge Press

MACMILLAN is a registered trademark of Macmillan General
Reference USA, Inc.
UNOFFICIAL GUIDE is a registered trademark of
Macmillan General Reference USA, Inc.

ISBN 0-02-863351-2

ISSN 1523-0651

Manufactured in the United States of America

10 9 8 7 6 5 4 3 2 1

Contents

List of Maps

Introduction

How Come "Unofficial"?

The author and researchers of this guide specifically and categorically declare that they are and always have been totally independent. The material in this guide originated with the authors and has not been reviewed, edited, or in any way approved by the companies whose travel products are discussed. The purpose of this guide is to provide you with the information necessary to tour central Florida with the greatest efficiency and economy, and with the least hassle and stress. In this guide we represent and serve you, the consumer. If a restaurant serves bad food, or a gift item is overpriced, or a certain ride isn't worth the wait, we can say so, and in the process we hope to make your visit more fun, efficient, and economical.

There's Another Whole World Out There

If you think that central Florida consists only of Walt Disney World, you're wrong. What's more, you're passing up some great fun and amazing sights. Admittedly, it's taken awhile, but Walt Disney World now has plenty of competition that measures up toe-to-toe. And though it may sound blasphemous to suggest a whole vacation in central Florida without setting foot on Disney property, it's not only possible, but also in many ways a fresh and appealing idea.

The big four non-Disney theme parks are Universal Studios Florida, Universal Studios Islands of Adventure, SeaWorld, and Busch Gardens. Each is unique. Universal Studios Florida, a longtime rival of the Disney-MGM Studios, draws its inspiration from movies and television and is every bit the equal of the Disney movie-theme park. Islands of Adventure is arguably the most modern, high tech theme park in the United States, featuring an all-star lineup of thrill rides that makes it the best park in Florida for older kids and young-at-heart adults. SeaWorld provides an incomparable glimpse into the world of marine mammals and fish, served up in a way that (for the most part) eliminates those never-ending lines. Finally, Busch Gardens, with its shows, zoo-logical exhibits, and knockout coasters, offers the most eclectic entertainment mix of any theme park we know. All four parks approximate, equal, or exceed the Disney standard without imi-tating Disney, successfully blending their own distinctive presen-tation and personality into every attraction.

In addition to the big four, there are three specialty parks that are also very worthy of your attention. Cypress Gardens combines stunning formal gardens with its signature water skiing shows. The Kennedy Space Center at Cape Canaveral provides an inside look at the past, present, and future of America's space program, while Gatorland showcases the alligator, one of the most ancient creatures on earth. All three offer an experience that is quite dif-ferent from a day at one of the big theme parks, including a respite from standing in line, all of the walking, and the frenetic pace.

But these are just for starters. In central Florida you'll also find a vibrant dinner theater scene, two excellent non-Disney water parks, two rocking nighttime entertainment complexes, great shopping, and some of the best hiking, biking, fishing, and canoe-ing opportunities available anywhere.

The Attraction That Ate Florida

Before Walt Disney World, Florida was a happy peninsula of many more-or-less equal tourist attractions. Distributed around the state in great profusion, they constituted the nation's most peren-nially appealing vacation opportunity. There was the Monkey Jungle, the Orchid Jungle, venerable Marineland, the St. Augus-tine Alligator Farm, Silver Springs, the Miami Wax Museum, the Sunken Gardens, the Coral Castle, and the Conch Train Tour. These, along with Cypress Gardens, Busch Gardens, and others, were the attractions that ruled Florida. Now, like so many dinosaurs, those remaining survive precariously on the droppings of the greatest beast of them all, Walt Disney World. Old stand-bys continue to welcome tourists, but when was the last time you planned your vacation around a visit to Jungle Larry's Safari Park?

When Walt Disney World arrived on the scene, Florida tourism changed forever. Before Disney (b.d.), southern Florida was the state's and the nation's foremost tourist destination. Throngs sunned on the beaches of Miami, Hollywood, and Fort Lauderdale, and patronized such nearby attractions as the Miami Serpentarium and the Parrot Jungle. Attractions in the Ocala and St. Augustine areas upstate hosted road travelers in great waves as they journeyed to and from southern Florida. At the time, Orlando was a sleepy central Florida town an hour's drive from Cypress Gardens, with practically no tourist appeal whatsoever.

Then came Disney, snapping up acres of farm- and swampland before anyone even knew who the purchaser was. Bargaining hard, Walt demanded improved highways, tax concessions, bargain financing, and community support. So successful had been his California Disneyland that whatever he requested, he received.

Generally approving, and hoping for a larger aggregate market, the existing Florida attractions failed to discern the cloud on the horizon. Walt had tipped his hand early, however, and all the cards were on the table. When Disney bought 27,500 central Florida acres, it was evident he didn't intend to raise cattle.

The Magic Kingdom opened on October 1, 1971, and was immediately successful. Hotel construction boomed in Orlando, Kissimmee, and around Walt Disney World. Major new attractions popped up along recently completed Interstate 4 to cash in on the tide of tourists arriving at Disney's latest wonder. Walt Disney World became a destination, and suddenly nobody cared as much about going to the beach. The Magic Kingdom was good for two days, and then you could enjoy the rest of the week at Sea World, Cypress Gardens, Circus World, Gatorland, Busch Gardens, the Stars Hall of Fame Wax Museum, and the Kennedy Space Center.

These attractions, all practically new and stretching from Florida's east coast to west coast, formed what would come to be called the Orlando Wall. Tourists no longer poured into Miami and Fort Lauderdale. Instead they stopped at the Orlando Wall and exhausted themselves and their dollars in the shiny attractions arrayed between Cape Canaveral and Tampa. In southern Florida, venerable attractions held on by a parrot feather and more than a few closed their doors. Flagship hotels on the fabled Gold Coast went bust or were converted into condominiums.

When Walt Disney World opened, the very definition of a tourist attraction changed. Setting standards for cleanliness, size, scope, grandeur, variety, and attention to detail, Disney World relegated the majority of Florida's headliner attractions to comparative insignificance almost overnight. Newer attractions such as Sea World and the vastly enlarged Busch Gardens successfully matched the standard Disney set. Cypress Gardens, Weeki Wachi, and Silver Springs expanded and modernized. Most other attractions, however, slipped into a limbo of diminished status. Far from being headliners or tourist destinations, they plugged along as local diversions, pulling in the curious, the bored, and the sunburned for two-hour excursions.

Many of the affected attractions were and are wonderful places to spend a day, but even collectively they don't command sufficient appeal to lure many tourists beyond the Wall. We recommend them, however, not only for their variety of high-quality offerings, but as a glimpse of Florida's golden age, a time of less sophisticated, less plastic pleasures before the Mouse. Take a day or two and drive three-and-a-half hours south of Orlando. Visit the Miami Seaquarium or Ocean World. Try Vizcaya, Fairchild Tropical Gardens, and Lion Country Safari. Drive Collins Avenue along the Gold Coast. You'll be glad you did.

When Epcot opened in Walt Disney World on October 1, 1982, another seismic shock reverberated throughout the Florida attractions industry. This time it wasn't only the smaller and more vulnerable attractions that were affected, but the newer large-scale attractions along the Orlando Wall. Suddenly, Disney World swallowed up another one or two days of each tourist's vacation week. When the Magic Kingdom stood alone, most visitors had three or four days remaining to sample other attractions. With the addition of Epcot, that time was cut to one or two days.

Disney ensured its market share by creating multiday admission passes, which allowed unlimited access to both the Magic Kingdom and Epcot. More cost-efficient than a one-day pass to a single park, these passes kept the guest on Disney turf for three to five days.

Kennedy Space Center and Sea World, by virtue of their very specialized products, continued to prosper after Epcot opened. Most other attractions were forced to focus on local markets. Some, like Busch Gardens, did very well, with increased local support replacing the decreased numbers of Walt Disney World–destination tourists coming over for the day. Others, like Cypress Gardens, suffered badly but worked diligently to improve their product. Some, like Circus World and the Hall of Fame Wax Museum, passed into history.

Though long an innovator, Disney turned in the mid-'80s to copying existing successful competitors. Except, copying is not exactly the right word. What Disney did was to take a competitor's concept, improve it, and reproduce it, in Disney style on a grand scale.

The first competitor to feel the heat was Sea World when Disney added The Living Seas pavilion to the Future World section of Epcot. Sea World, however, had killer whales, the Shark Encounter, and sufficient corporate resources to remain pre-eminent among marine exhibits. Still, many Disney patrons willingly substituted a visit to The Living Seas for a visit to Sea World.

One of Disney's own products was threatened when the Wet 'n Wild water theme park took aim at the older and smaller but more aesthetically pleasing River Country. Never one to take a challenge sitting down, Disney responded in 1989 with the opening of Typhoon Lagoon, then the world's largest swimming theme park.

Also in 1989, Disney opened Pleasure Island, a one-admission, multi-nightclub entertainment complex patterned on Orlando's successful Church Street Station. In the years it has operated, Pleasure Island has robbed Church Street Station of much of its tourist traffic.

In the same year, Walt Disney World opened Disney-MGM Studios, a combination working motion picture and television production complex and theme park. Copying the long-lauded Universal Studios tour in southern California, Disney-MGM Studios was speeded into operation after Universal announced its plans for a central Florida park.

Disney-MGM Studios, however, affected much more than Universal's plans. With the opening of Disney-MGM, the 3-Day World Passport was discontinued. Instead, Disney patrons were offered a single-day pass or the more economical multiday passports, good for either four or five days. With three theme parks on a multiday pass, plus two swimming parks, several golf courses, various lakes, and a nighttime entertainment complex, Disney effectively swallowed up the average family's entire vacation. Break away to Sea World or the Kennedy Space Center for the day? How about a day at the ocean (remember the ocean?) Fat chance.

In 1995, Disney opened Blizzard Beach, a third swimming theme park, and began plans for a fourth major theme park, the Animal Kingdom, designed to compete directly with Busch Gardens. During the same year, the first phase of Disney's All-Star resorts came on-line, featuring (by Disney standards) budget accommodations. The location and rates of the All-Star resorts were intended to capture the market of the smaller independent and chain hotels along US 192. Disney even discussed constructing a monorail to the airport so that visitors won't have to set foot in Orlando.

As time passed, Disney continued to consolidate its hold. With the opening of Disney's BoardWalk, Fantasia Gardens miniature golf, the Walt Disney World Speedway in 1996, Disney's Wide World of Sports, Disney's West Side shopping and entertainment district, and a new convention center in 1997, and the Animal Kingdom in 1998, Disney attracted armies of central Floridians to compensate for decreased tourist traffic during off-season. And for people who can never get enough, there is the town of Celebration, a Disney residential land development project where home buyers can live in Disney-designed houses in Disney-designed neighborhoods, protected by Disney-designed security.

In 1999, however, for the first time in many years, the initiative passed to Disney's competitors. Universal Studios Florida became a bona fide destination with the opening of its second major theme park, Islands of Adventure, and on-property hotels. Sea World likewise announced a second park, scheduled to open in 2000, and Busch Gardens turned up the heat with the addition of new roller coasters. The latest additions bring Busch Gardens' total to six coasters, making them the roller coaster capital of Florida. Giving Disney some of its own medicine, Busch, Sea World, and Universal combined with Wet 'n Wild and Cypress Gardens to offer multiday passes good at any of the parks. While it may be too early to say that Disney's hegemony is at an end, one thing's for sure: Disney's not the only 800 pound gorilla on the block anymore.

All this competition, of course, is good for central Florida, and it's good for you. The time, money, and creative energy invested in developing ever-better parks and attractions is mind boggling. Nobody, including Disney, can rest on their laurels in this market. And as for you, you're certain to find something new and amazing on very visit.

TRYING TO REASON WITH THE TOURIST SEASON

Central Florida theme parks and attractions are busiest Christmas Day through New Year's Day. Thanksgiving weekend, the week of Washington's birthday, Martin Luther King holiday weekend, spring break for colleges, and the two weeks around Easter are also extremely busy. What does "busy" mean? As many as 92,000 people have toured the Magic Kingdom alone on a single day during these peak times! While this level of attendance isn't typical, it is possible, and only the ignorant or foolish challenge the major Florida theme parks at their peak periods.

The least busy time extends from after the Thanksgiving weekend until the week before Christmas. The next slowest times are November up to the weekend preceding Thanksgiving, January 4th through the first week of February, and the week after Easter through early June. Late February, March, and early April are dicey. Crowds ebb and flow according to spring break schedules and the timing of Presidents' Day weekend. Though crowds have grown markedly in September and October as a result of special promotions aimed at locals and the international market, these months continue to be good for weekday touring.

It Takes More Than One Book To Do the Job Right

We've been covering central Florida tourism for over 20 years. We began by lumping everything into one guidebook, but that was when the Magic Kingdom was the only theme park at Walt Disney World, at the very beginning of the boom that has made central Florida the most visited tourist destination on earth. As central Florida grew, so did our guide, until eventually we needed to split the tome into smaller, more in-depth (and more portable) volumes. The result is a small library of six titles, designed to work both individually and together. All six provide specialized information tailored to very specific central Florida and Walt Disney World visitors. Although some tips (like arriving at the theme parks early) are echoed or elaborated in the all the guides, most of the information in each book is unique.

The Unofficial Guide To Walt Disney World is the centerpiece of our central Florida coverage because, well . . ., Walt Disney World is the centerpiece of most central Florida vacations. *The Unofficial Guide To Walt Disney World* is evaluative, comprehensive, and instructive, the ultimate planning tool for a successful Walt Disney World vacation. *The Unofficial Guide To Walt Disney World* is supplemented and augmented by five additional titles, including this guide:

Mini-Mickey: The Pocket-Sized Unofficial Guide to Walt Disney World by Bob Sehlinger; 320 pages; $10.95

Inside Disney: The Incredible Story of Walt Disney World and the Man Behind the Mouse by Eve Zibart; 240 pages; $9.95

The Unofficial Guide To Walt Disney World With Kids by Bob Sehlinger; 240 pages; $11.95

The Unofficial Guide to Walt Disney World for Grown-Ups by Eve Zibart; 200 pages; $9.95

Beyond Disney, The Unofficial Guide To Universal, SeaWorld, and Central Florida by Bob Sehlinger and Amber Morris; 184 pages; $9.95

Mini-Mickey is a nifty, portable, "Cliff Notes" version of *The Unofficial Guide to Walt Disney World.* Updated annually, it distills information from this comprehensive guide to help short-stay or last-minute visitors decide quickly how to plan their limited hours at Disney World. *Inside Disney* is a behind-the-scenes unauthorized history of Walt Disney World, and it is loaded with all the amazing facts and great stories that we can't squeeze into *The Unofficial Guide To Walt Disney World. The Unofficial Guide to Walt Disney World For Grown-Ups* helps adults traveling without children make the most of their Disney vacation, while *The Unofficial Guide To Walt Disney World With Kids* presents a wealth of planning and touring tips for a successful Disney family vacation. Finally, this guide, *Beyond Disney,* is a complete consumer guide to the non-Disney attractions, restaurants, outdoor recreation, and nightlife in Orlando and central Florida. All of the guides are available from Macmillan Travel and at most bookstores.

Letters and Comments from Readers

Many of those who use the Unofficial Guides write us to make comments or share their own strategies for visiting central Florida. We appreciate all such input, both positive and critical, and encourage our readers to continue writing. Readers' comments and observations are frequently incorporated into revised editions of the Unofficial Guide and have contributed immeasurably to its improvement. If you write us or return our reader survey form, you can rest assured that we won't release your name and address to any mailing list companies, direct mail advertisers, or other third party.

How to Write the Author:

Bob Sehlinger and Amber Morris
The Unofficial Guides
P.O. Box 43673
Birmingham, AL 35243

When you write, put your address on both your letter and envelope. Sometimes the two get separated. It is also a good idea to include your phone number. And remember, as travel writers, we're often out of the office for long periods of time, so forgive us if our response is slow.

Part One

Busch Gardens

Spanning 335 acres, Busch Gardens combines elements of a zoo and theme park. A haven for thrill-ride fanatics, the park offers two roller coasters that are consistently rated among the top five in the country. Busch Gardens is more than thrill fare, however, with beautiful landscape, excellent shows, and a really wonderful children's play area.

With the wildlife of Disney's Animal Kingdom and the thrills of Universal Studios' Islands of Adventure, some may wonder why leave Orlando for a day at Busch Gardens in Tampa? For those who love roller coasters, Busch Gardens boasts five, three in the "super-coaster" category. No other area attraction can top that in terms of thrills. Nor can it be matched in its ability to offer a balanced day of fun for all ages. Those who shy away from roller coasters will find plenty to do at the park with its abundance of animal exhibits, children's rides, gardens, shows, and shops.

In addition, the drive is easy—about an hour and a half. And with Florida's fickle weather, it could be raining in Orlando, but bright and sunny in Tampa, so it's a good idea to check the weather if you're rained out of O-town. Of course, this holds true in reverse, and, unlike Disney where most of the rides are indoors, any rain will cause the closing of most of the rides at Busch Gardens. The park is also minutes away from the sandy white beaches of St. Petersburg and Tampa Bay, an often overlooked advantage.

GETTING THERE

Busch Gardens is approximately 70 miles from Walt Disney World. The trip should take about an hour and a half, depending on traffic and the construction that plagues I-4. The best way to get there is via I-75. Driving west on I-4, there are signs for Busch Gardens, but we recommend ignoring them to avoid a long journey through Tampa city streets. Proceed instead to the junction of I-75 and go north. Exit at Busch Boulevard (exit 33) and follow the signs. Parking is $5 in a lot across the street from the park (trams are provided) and $10 in a preferred lot closer to the main entrance.

ADMISSION PRICES

Before purchasing tickets to Busch Gardens, consider some of the choices below, which are similar to the options offered by sister park SeaWorld. As with SeaWorld, the best option for most visitors is a one-day pass. If you're planning to spend time at other Orlando theme parks, however, consider the FlexTicket or the Adventure Passport, which include admission to SeaWorld. Discounts are available for AAA members, disabled visitors, senior citizens, and military personal.

One-day Pass
Adults: $44 plus tax
Children (ages 3–9): $35
Children under age 3: Free

Two-day Pass
A "next day" ticket can be purchased for $10.95 at Guest Relations. Buy the ticket at any time during your first visit. It can only be used the next consecutive day.

Adventure Passport
(Five consecutive days at Busch Gardens and SeaWorld)
Adults: $79
Children: $64

Orlando FlexTicket
(Ten consecutive days at Universal Studios Florida, Islands of Adventure, SeaWorld, Wet 'n Wild, and Busch Gardens)
Adults: $196.95
Children (ages 3–9): $157.95

ARRIVING

Normal park hours are 9:30 a.m. to 6 p.m., with extended morning and evening hours during summer and holidays. (Unlike other

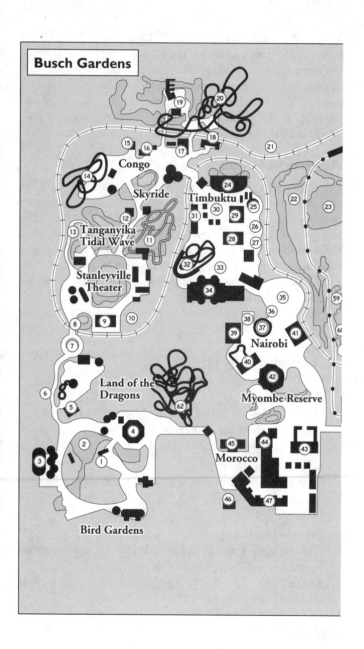

Busch Gardens

Congo

Skyride

Timbuktu

Tanganyika
Tidal Wave

Stanleyville
Theater

Nairobi

Land of the
Dragons

Myombe Reserve

Morocco

Bird Gardens

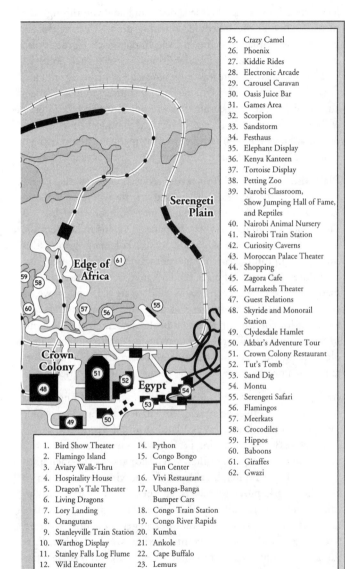

25. Crazy Camel
26. Phoenix
27. Kiddie Rides
28. Electronic Arcade
29. Carousel Caravan
30. Oasis Juice Bar
31. Games Area
32. Scorpion
33. Sandstorm
34. Festhaus
35. Elephant Display
36. Kenya Kanteen
37. Tortoise Display
38. Petting Zoo
39. Narobi Classroom,
    Show Jumping Hall of Fame,
    and Reptiles
40. Nairobi Animal Nursery
41. Nairobi Train Station
42. Curiosity Caverns
43. Moroccan Palace Theater
44. Shopping
45. Zagora Cafe
46. Marrakesh Theater
47. Guest Relations
48. Skyride and Monorail
    Station
49. Clydesdale Hamlet
50. Akbar's Adventure Tour
51. Crown Colony Restaurant
52. Tut's Tomb
53. Sand Dig
54. Montu
55. Serengeti Safari
56. Flamingos
57. Meerkats
58. Crocodiles
59. Hippos
60. Baboons
61. Giraffes
62. Gwazi

Serengeti Plain

Edge of Africa

Crown Colony

Egypt

1. Bird Show Theater
2. Flamingo Island
3. Aviary Walk-Thru
4. Hospitality House
5. Dragon's Tale Theater
6. Living Dragons
7. Lory Landing
8. Orangutans
9. Stanleyville Train Station
10. Warthog Display
11. Stanley Falls Log Flume
12. Wild Encounter
13. Orchid Canyon
14. Python
15. Congo Bongo
    Fun Center
16. Vivi Restaurant
17. Ubanga-Banga
    Bumper Cars
18. Congo Train Station
19. Congo River Rapids
20. Kumba
21. Ankole
22. Cape Buffalo
23. Lemurs
24. Dolphin Theater

local attractions, Busch Gardens does not allow you through the turnstiles before the scheduled opening time.) Visiting during peak seasons equals waiting in long lines. Busch Gardens also draws crowds of locals, so avoid visiting on weekends or holidays.

Even when crowds are low, it requires a lot of planning and hustling to see Busch Gardens in one day. Of course, group age ranges and personal tastes will eliminate some rides and exhibits. Groups without children, for instance, don't need to budget time for kiddie rides. However, even selective touring many not afford enough time to enjoy the park fully. Following are a few tips that may help:

Plan Ahead   Many visitors seeing a Busch Gardens map crammed full of rides and exhibits for the first time develop a glazed look in their eyes and begin a crazed tour. Somehow, we doubt if these folk see even half of what the park offers. Instead, determine in advance what you really want to see. For many groups this involves compromise: Parents may not want to spend as much time as children on rides, whereas the kids may want to steer clear of many of the zoological exhibits. If children are old enough, we recommend splitting up after determining a few meetings times and locations for checking in throughout the day. Alternately, parents may want to plan kids' rides around the live entertainment schedule, placing children safely in line and then attending a performance of a nearby show while the youngsters wait and ride.

Arrive Early   As with other central Florida attractions, this is the single most effective strategy for efficient touring and avoiding long waits in line. Leave Orlando around 7 a.m. to arrive a little before 8:30 a.m. during peak season. Give yourself an extra half an hour during other times, when the park doesn't open until 9:30 a.m. Have a quick breakfast before leaving, or in the car to save time. Park, purchase tickets, and be at the turnstile ready to roll when the attraction opens at either 9 or 9:30 a.m. If you're doing the roller-coaster circuit, we suggest you plan to head straight to Gwazi, then to Montu, saving Kumba for last. First thing in the morning, there should be no lines and relatively few people. These same three attractions experienced in one hour in the morning could require more than three hours after 11:30 a.m.

Be Ready to Walk and Walk and Walk   Busch Gardens is huge and requires lots of walking. Definitely get strollers for little ones and consider wheelchairs for others who will tire quickly. In addition, have all members in your party grab a park map and show schedule (which are frustratingly not combined as at most other attractions). With no central hub and few connecting walkways, the park is very difficult to maneuver, and you'll appreciate the navigational help of your entire gang.

Avoid Bottlenecks An early arrival will help you avoid the bottlenecks at most of the major attractions. As for other smaller rides, if there's a line, don't wait. Go see a show or visit the animal exhibits, which usually have no wait. Then return to the rides later in the day, when lines should subside.

CONTACTING BUSCH GARDENS

For more information, call (813) 987-5082. If you'd like to avoid the charge of a long-distance call, try (800) 4ADVENTURE, but be prepared to spend a little more time because you'll need to wade through a menu of all the other Anheuser-Busch theme parks. Or visit the Busch Gardens Web site at www.buschgardens.com. An animal information database also can be found at www.buschgardens.org.

Attractions

MOROCCO

Marrakesh Theater/*American Jukebox*

What It Is: Song and dance show
Scope & Scale: Major attraction
When to Go: Check daily entertainment schedule
Author's Rating: Amusing and entertaining; ★★★
Overall Appeal by Age Group:

Pre-School	Grade School	Teens	Young Adults	Over 30	Senior Citizens
★★½	★★★	★★½	★★★	★★★	★★★½

Duration of Show: 25 minutes

Description & Comments A talented cast sings and dances to songs from the 1950s to the '90s in this lively show. Costumes range from poodle skirts to bell-bottoms, and the revolving set changes with each decade of music. Highlights include an Elvis number in which a run-in with screaming "fans" leaving the singer in little more than undergarments and his blue suede shoes; the entire male cast dressing up as the Village People for YMCA; and a male cast member masterfully belting out country favorites, including *Don't Rock the Jukebox*.

Touring Tips   Rows of wrought-iron patio seats fill this outdoor theater. They are not on an incline, and it is difficult to see the stage from the back. Arrive ten minutes early to get the best seats near the front of the house. Also, rows to the right or left of the stage don't fill up as quickly and offer great views.

Moroccan Palace Theater/*Hollywood Live on Ice*

What It Is: Ice-skating show

Scope & Scale: Headliner

When to Go: Check daily entertainment schedule

Author's Rating: Impressive; ★★★

Overall Appeal by Age Group:

Pre-School	Grade School	Teens	Young Adults	Over 30	Senior Citizens
★★★	★★★	★★★	★★★½	★★★½	★★★½

Duration of Show: 30 minutes

Description & Comments   Most theme park ice-skating shows are a bit hokey, like *Hot Noveau Ice* at Cypress Gardens, but not this one. It's a well-choreographed glimpse of Hollywood history performed by an extremely talented cast. In one of the best moments, a couple evokes the smooth moves of Fred Astaire and Ginger Rogers with graceful, innovative lifts and jumps. In another elaborate scene—complete with a hovering helicopter and a mannequin hang-gliding over the audience—Agent 007 battles bad guys to save the girl. Other highlights include a tribute to silent films and the horror genre, and a solo of *Somewhere Over the Rainbow* by a Dorothy look-a-like performed in red-sequined skates.

Touring Tips   Don't sit in the first five to seven rows if you don't want to get splashed by a storm effect for a *Singin' in the Rain* number.

CROWN COLONY

Skyride

What It Is: Scenic transportation to Stanleyville

Scope & Scale: Minor attraction

When to Go: Lines can be long in the afternoon

Author's Rating: Great way to see the Serengeti Plain area; ★★½

Overall Appeal by Age Group:

Pre-School	Grade School	Teens	Young Adults	Over 30	Senior Citizens
★★	★★½	★★	★★½	★★½	★★½

Duration of Ride: 4 minutes

Description & Comments This slow-moving, four-person, chair-lift type ride travels to Stanleyville. It offers a great look at the animals on the Serengeti Plain, as well as a neat perspective of the nearby roller coasters. You can board here or in Stanleyville, but you cannot stay on for a round-trip.

Touring Tips Unless lines are short, this ride takes much longer than walking. However, because the Busch Gardens monorail has been closed indefinitely, only this and the train offer views of the Serengeti Plain.

Clydesdale Hamlet

What It Is: Horse stable

Scope & Scale: Diversion

When to Go: Anytime

Author's Rating: Great for kids; ★★

Overall Appeal by Age Group:

Pre-School	Grade School	Teens	Young Adults	Over 30	Senior Citizens
★★½	★★½	★½	★★	★★	★★½

Description & Comments This blue-roofed, white stable is home to several Clydesdales, huge and beautiful draft horses that are the Anheuser-Busch mascots.

Touring Tips These horses are truly amazing to look at, and kids will really enjoy this, but don't waste time here if you're trying to rush through all the coasters and water rides.

Edge of Africa

What It Is: Walking tour of animal habitats

Scope & Scale: Headliner

When to Go: Crowds are minuscule in the afternoon, and the
   animals are fairly active

Author's Rating: Good presentation; ★★★½

Overall Appeal by Age Group:

Pre-School	Grade School	Teens	Young Adults	Over 30	Senior Citizens
★★★	★★★½	★★★	★★★½	★★★½	★★★½

Description & Comments This walking safari features hippopotamus, giraffes, lions, baboons, meerkats, hyenas, and vul-
tures in naturalistic habitats. The area was designed for up-close
viewing, many times with just a pane of glass between you and
the animals. Of note are the hippopotamus exhibit and the hyena
area. The hippopotamus wade in five-foot-deep water filled with
colorful fish, all visible through the glass wall. In the hyena habitat, open safari vehicles are built into the glass, offering a great
photo location if you climb in when the animals come near.

Touring Tips Animals are most active during feedings, but these
are not regularly scheduled, so the animals don't fall into a pat-
tern that would not exist in the wild. Employees in the area are
usually willing to tell you feeding times for the day. It might be a
hike to return to this area, but seeing the lions chomp into raw
meat with their large teeth is definitely worth it.

There is a hidden entrance to this area between Tut's Tomb
and the rest rooms near Montu. This is useful if you ride the roller
coaster before seeing the animals.

Serengeti Safari Tour

What It Is: Guided tour

Scope & Scale: Major attraction

When to Go: Call reservation number for a schedule

Special Comments: Costs $20 for everyone age 5 and older

Author's Rating: Nice, but might be too expensive for the average
   visitor; ★★★½

Overall Appeal by Age Group:

Pre-School	Grade School	Teens	Young Adults	Over 30	Senior Citizens
★★★	★★★½	★★★	★★★½	★★★½	★★★½

Duration of Tour: 30 minutes

Description & Comments If you don't mind spending the extra $20, this guided tour of the Serengeti Plain provides amazing close encounters with the animals. You'll board a flatbed truck and head into an area where no other visitors are allowed. The highlight of the trip is feeding the giraffes. It's amazing to watch their long tongues remove all the leaves from a prickly branch while adeptly avoiding the thorns.

Touring Tips Only 20 people can fit on the truck, so it's a good idea to make reservations in advance. Call (813) 987-5212 for reservations and more information.

EGYPT

Akbar's Adventure Tours

What It Is: Simulator ride

Scope & Scale: Major attraction

When to Go: Not immediately following a *Hollywood Live on Ice* show

Special Comments: Riders must be at least 48 inches tall

Author's Rating: A good thrill with lots of gags; ★★★

Overall Appeal by Age Group:

Pre-School	Grade School	Teens	Young Adults	Over 30	Senior Citizens
†	★★★	★★★	★★★	★★★	★★½

†Preschoolers are generally too short to ride.

Duration of Ride: 10 minutes

Description & Comments This simulator ride stars Martin Short as an Egyptian marketplace peddler looking to make a buck from hordes of tourists by offering rides on his new contraption. Similar to story lines on most Orlando simulator rides, something goes hilariously wrong, creating a memorable ride through sandy deserts, Egyptian tombs, and crowded markets.

Touring Tips Though older kids will appreciate the humor and sight gags of this ride, it contains several intense *Indiana Jones*–like effects that will definitely scare young children.

Tut's Tomb

What It Is: Walking tour of a re-created tomb

Scope & Scale: Diversion

When to Go: Anytime, don't wait if there's a line

Author's Rating: Interesting, but not necessarily worth the time;
★★

Overall Appeal by Age Group:

Pre-School	Grade School	Teens	Young Adults	Over 30	Senior Citizens
★	★½	★½	★★	★★	★★½

Duration of Tour: 10 minutes

Description & Comments   The spirit of King Tut leads you on a tour of this re-creation of his tomb. The narration features information about the artifacts and his life. Objects on display include replicas of Tut's large throne, chariot, and golden sculpted coffin, as well as urns containing his internal organs.

Touring Tips   This air-conditioned attraction does provide a break from the heat, but should be skipped if you're in a hurry. It is a perfect time-killer for visitors who are waiting for the rest of their party to ride Montu.

Montu

What It Is: Inverted, steel "super" roller coaster

Scope & Scale: Super headliner

When to Go: Before 10 a.m. or after 3 p.m.

Special Comments: Riders must be at least 54 inches tall

Author's Rating: Incredible; ★★★★

Overall Appeal by Age Group:

Pre-School	Grade School	Teens	Young Adults	Over 30	Senior Citizens
†	★★★★	★★★★	★★★★	★★★½	★★

†Preschoolers are generally too short to ride.

Duration of Ride: About 3 minutes

Loading Speed: Quick

Description & Comments   Seats hang below the track and riders feet dangle on this intense inverted roller coaster, which is among the top five in the country and the best we've ever ridden. The fast-paced but extremely smooth ride begins with a 13-story drop. Riders' are then hurled through a 104-foot inverted vertical loop. Speeds reach 60 mph as riders are accelerated through more dizzying loops and twists, including an "Immelman," an inverse loop named after a German fighter pilot.

Touring Tips   Ride in the morning to avoid waits that can be as long as an hour. We suggest you hurry to Gwazi when the park opens and then head here. If you don't arrive early, however, don't be discouraged. As many as 32 riders can pile on to each train, so even the longest line will move quickly and steadily.

If you have time, ride twice, first near the back of the train and then in the front row. In the back, you'll glimpse a sea of dangling feet in front of you and be surprised by each twist and turn because you can't see where the track is headed, just legs swooping through the air. Riding in the front gives you a clear, unobstructed view of everything around you, including the huge trees dozens of feet below you on the first drop. Look for the special "front seat" queue once you enter the load station. The wait for the front is usually an extra 20 minutes.

Be sure to look down as you exit the station house to catch a glimpse of some surprise spectators.

NAIROBI

Myombe Reserve

What It Is: Gorilla and ape habitat
Scope & Scale: Major attraction
When to Go: In the morning
Author's Rating: Great theming, informative; ★★★
Overall Appeal by Age Group:

Pre-School	Grade School	Teens	Young Adults	Over 30	Senior Citizens
★★★	★★★	★★½	★★★	★★★	★★★

Description & Comments   A mist-filled path through lush landscape leads you to this beautiful habitat filled with thick vegetation, waterfalls, and marshlands. The first section is home to several chimpanzees, which can usually be found romping through the trees and greenery. The second area features large gorillas. Only one or two of the animals are regularly visible, but at least one usually can be found napping in front of the glass. Two overhead monitors play a video full of interesting information about each of the animals in the habitat, including how they interact with each other. Chalkboards throughout the exhibit provide facts and figures about the animals.

Touring Tips   The animals are usually most active before 11 a.m. After riding Montu you can snake through this exhibit, which exits into Nairobi, on your way to Kumba.

Bronze sculptures of gorillas and chimpanzees placed throughout the exhibit provide some fun photo opportunities. Climb onto the giant gorilla at the entrance or join the train of chimpanzees combing through each other's hair for a unique snapshot.

Trans-Veldt Railroad

What It Is: Tour through Serengeti Plain and around park with two stops

Scope & Scale: Minor attraction

When to Go: Afternoon

Author's Rating: Relaxing; ★★★

Overall Appeal by Age Group:

Pre-School	Grade School	Teens	Young Adults	Over 30	Senior Citizens
★★★	★★★	★★★	★★★	★★★	★★★

Duration of Ride: 10 minutes through animal area exiting at next station; 30 minutes round-trip

Description & Comments   Riding this train gives your feet a break and provides the best view of the animals along the Serengeti Plain. Because it's quite slow, we don't recommend it as an alternate means of transportation, but the ten-minute trip from the Nairobi station through the Serengeti Plain to the Congo station is worth the time if you're not racing to ride the coasters.

Touring Tips   Have your favorite animal sounds ready. Many of the narrators invite you to whoop it up as the train enters a tunnel in the Serengeti Plain. It's lots of fun and sounds just like a jungle full of wild creatures—with a train chugging through, of course.

Animal Nursery

What It Is: Newborns on display

Scope & Scale: Minor attraction

When to Go: Anytime

Author's Rating: Adorable; ★★½
Overall Appeal by Age Group:

Pre-School	Grade School	Teens	Young Adults	Over 30	Senior Citizens
★★½	★★½	★★	★★½	★★½	★★★

Description & Comments Busch Gardens is home to more than 2,700 animals, who often give birth. The park also rescues ill or orphaned animal infants, many of which are endangered. Walk by large windows in this animal nursery for a glimpse of some of these incredibly cute and cuddly babies. The quality of the experience depends on which animals have recently been born. During one visit we saw some adorable tiger cubs and scrawny but cute baby birds feeding from an eyedropper.

Touring Tips A sign near the entrance usually explains which animals are on display. Have a look before you waste time touring if nothing interests you.

Petting Zoo

What It Is: Animal petting area
Scope & Scale: Minor attraction
When to Go: Anytime
Author's Rating: Fun; ★★½
Overall Appeal by Age Group:

Pre-School	Grade School	Teens	Young Adults	Over 30	Senior Citizens
★★★	★★★	★★	★★½	★★	★★

Description & Comments Grab a small plastic brush and groom one of the numerous goats roaming this exhibit. There are also bunnies and other animals in pens surrounding the goat area.

Touring Tips Avoid visiting when as many as 380 people dump off a train entering the Nairobi station. Wait a bit for the area to clear.

Elephant Display

What It Is: Elephant habitat
Scope & Scale: Minor attraction
When to Go: During enrichment times

Author's Rating: ★★½
Overall Appeal by Age Group:

Pre-School	Grade School	Teens	Young Adults	Over 30	Senior Citizens
★★★	★★★	★★	★★½	★★★	★★★

Description & Comments   Endangered Asian elephants roam a dry dirt landscape. A large pool is deep enough for these huge animals to submerge themselves to escape the Florida heat.

Touring Tips   Visit during enrichment times when trainers interact with the animals, sometimes hosing them down. The daily entertainment schedule doesn't list enrichment times for all animals, so you may need to check a detailed sign at the exhibit.

TIMBUKTU

Sandstorm

What It Is: Carnival ride
Scope & Scale: Minor attraction
When to Go: Anytime
Special Comments: Riders must be at least 48 inches tall
Author's Rating: Amusing, but not worth a long wait; ★★½
Overall Appeal by Age Group:

Pre-School	Grade School	Teens	Young Adults	Over 30	Senior Citizens
†	★★★	★★½	★★½	★★½	★★

†Preschoolers are generally too short to ride.

Duration of Ride: Approximately 3 minutes
Loading Speed: Slow

Description & Comments   This is Busch Gardens' version of a midway ride commonly known as the Scrambler. Two to three riders sit in an enclosed car. Four of the cars rotate on one of six arms that circle a central pedestal.

Touring Tips   Though fun, this ride is nothing special. Skip it if lines are long.

Scorpion

What It Is: Roller coaster
Scope & Scale: Headliner

When to Go: After 2 p.m.

Special Comments: Riders must be at least 42 inches tall

Author's Rating: Quick, but exciting; ★★★

Overall Appeal by Age Group:

Pre-School	Grade School	Teens	Young Adults	Over 30	Senior Citizens
†	★★★	★★★	★★★	★★★	★★

†Preschoolers are generally too short to ride.

Duration of Ride: Approximately 1½ minutes

Description & Comments This coaster pales in comparison to big sisters Kumba and Montu. But at speeds of 50 mph with a 360° vertical loop and three 360° spirals, it's nothing to sneeze at.

Touring Tips Lines will be long for this attraction; because it doesn't have the high capacity of Kumba or Montu, they move slowly. Save it for the afternoon, when the wait should be shorter.

Kiddie Rides

What It Is: Pint-sized carnival rides

Scope & Scale: Minor attractions

When to Go: Anytime

Author's Rating: Good diversion for children; ★★½

Overall Appeal by Age Group:

Pre-School	Grade School	Teens	Young Adults	Over 30	Senior Citizens
★★★	†	†	†	†	†

†Not designed for older kids and adults.

Description & Comments These attractions are nothing fancy, but help kids that aren't old enough to ride the thrillers feel like they aren't being left out.

Touring Tips These rides are strategically placed near the adult attractions in this area (Scorpion and Phoenix), so one parent can keep the kids occupied while another rides.

Phoenix

What It Is: Swinging pendulum ride

Scope & Scale: Minor attraction

When to Go: Anytime

Special Comments: Riders must be at least 48 inches tall; not for those who get motion sickness

Author's Rating: Dizzying; ★★½

Overall Appeal by Age Group:

Pre-School	Grade School	Teens	Young Adults	Over 30	Senior Citizens
†	★★★	★★★	★★½	★★½	★

†Preschoolers are generally too short to ride.

Duration of Ride: 5 minutes

Description & Comments   A large wooden boat swings back and forth, starting slowly, then gaining speed before making a complete circle with passengers hanging upside down.

Touring Tips   Remove glasses and anything in your pockets to avoid losing them when the boat is suspended upside down for several seconds.

Dolphin Theater/*Dolphins of the Deep*

What It Is: Dolphin and sea lion show

Scope & Scale: Major attraction

When to Go: Check daily entertainment schedule

Author's Rating: Very nice; ★★★

Overall Appeal by Age Group:

Pre-School	Grade School	Teens	Young Adults	Over 30	Senior Citizens
★★★	★★★	★★½	★★★	★★★	★★★½

Duration of Show: 25 minutes

Description & Comments   Busch Gardens has received three dolphins and two sea lions from sister park SeaWorld. The dolphins, Bud, Mich, and Doulie, are named after some of park owner Anheuser-Busch's brew. The sea lions have the same stage names as those at SeaWorld—Clyde and Seamore. The show isn't as well produced as the SeaWorld shows, but it is nonetheless entertaining. It features some great pop music, which helps create one of the best moments—an amusing Blues Brother shtick with a dancing sea lion.

Touring Tips   This show is extremely cute, but if you're going to be visiting SeaWorld, you may want to consider skipping it in favor of riding attractions not found at the marine-life park.

If you'd like a snack, there's a refreshment booth selling popcorn, ice cream, and drinks in the rear of this open-air stadium.

CONGO

Ubanga-Banga Bumper Cars

What It Is: Bumper car ride
Scope & Scale: Minor attraction
When to Go: Anytime
Author's Rating: Fun; ★★½
Overall Appeal by Age Group:

Pre-School	Grade School	Teens	Young Adults	Over 30	Senior Citizens
★★★	★★★	★★★	★★½	★★	★

Duration of Ride: Approximately 2 minutes, depending on park attendance

Description & Comments Basic carnival bumper car ride.

Touring Tips Don't waste time waiting in the usually long line for this attraction if you're doing the roller-coaster circuit. However, because this attraction is right next to Kumba, it is a perfect place for kids and others in your group to wait for those braving the coaster.

Kumba

What It Is: Steel "super" roller coaster
Scope & Scale: Super headliner
When to Go: Before 11 a.m. or after 1:30 p.m.
Special Comments: Riders must be at least 54 inches tall
Author's Rating: Excellent; ★★★★
Overall Appeal by Age Group:

Pre-School	Grade School	Teens	Young Adults	Over 30	Senior Citizens
†	★★★★	★★★★	★★★★	★★★★	★★

†Preschoolers are generally too short to ride.

Duration of Ride: Approximately 3 minutes

Description & Comments Just like sister ride Montu, Kumba is one of the top roller coasters in the country. Unlike Montu,

Kumba's ride vehicles sit on top of the track as it roars through 3,900 feet of twists and loops. Reaching speeds of 60 mph, Kumba is certainly fast, but it also offers an incredibly smooth ride. Thrilling elements include a diving loop, a camelback with a 360° spiral, and a 108-foot vertical loop.

Touring Tips   Ride Gwazi and Montu first, then head to Kumba. Just like Montu, as many as 32 riders can brave Kumba at once, so even if there is a line, the wait shouldn't be unbearable.

Congo River Rapids

What It Is: Whitewater raft ride

Scope & Scale: Headliner

When to Go: After 4 p.m.

Special Comments: You will get soaked

Author's Rating: A great time, but not worth more than a 45-minute wait; ★★★½

Overall Appeal by Age Group:

Pre-School	Grade School	Teens	Young Adults	Over 30	Senior Citizens
★★★½	★★★½	★★★½	★★★½	★★★	★★½

Duration of Ride: 4 ½–5 minutes

Loading Speed: Slow to moderate

Description & Comments   Whitewater raft rides have become somewhat of a theme park standard. Nevertheless, this attraction is fun and exciting. Twelve riders sit on a circular rubber raft as they float down a man-made river, jostling and spinning in the waves and rapids. Boats are not on a track, and there's no telling where they will go. Part of the fun is waiting to see which riders will get drenched when their side of the boat happens to plunge into an enormous wave.

Touring Tips   Long lines for this attraction are inevitable. We recommend you ride the roller coasters first, saving this attraction for later in the afternoon.

You can get drenched on this attraction. A rain poncho will help somewhat, but will not protect you entirely. If you don't have rain gear, try to remove as much clothing as possible; definitely remove your socks, which are incredibly uncomfortable when soggy. Incidentally, it takes a little over two hours to dry out on a sunny winter day and bit less during the summer.

Claw Island Tigers

What It Is: Tiger habitat

Scope & Scale: Minor attraction

When to Go: Animals are most active in the morning, but always visible

Author's Rating: Beautiful creatures; ★★★

Overall Appeal by Age Group:

Pre-School	Grade School	Teens	Young Adults	Over 30	Senior Citizens
★★★	★★★	★★½	★★★	★★★	★★★

Description & Comments   A lush, sunken island is home to several Bengal tigers, one of which is a rare white tiger. The island is surrounded by a lagoon fed by a waterfall.

Touring Tips   The animals are visible, but are usually napping in the afternoon. Stop by quickly on your morning walk to Kumba to possibly catch them in action. The animals are also more lively during scheduled enrichment times. Check the daily entertainment guide or a listing at the habitat.

Python

What It Is: Roller coaster

Scope & Scale: Headliner

When to Go: After 3 p.m.

Special Comments: Riders must be at least 48 inches tall

Author's Rating: A quick adrenaline rush; ★★★

Overall Appeal by Age Group:

Pre-School	Grade School	Teens	Young Adults	Over 30	Senior Citizens
†	★★★½	★★★½	★★★	★★★	★★

†Preschoolers are generally too short to ride.

Duration of Ride: Approximately 1 minute

Description & Comments   At less than a third the size of Kumba, the Python offers a brief thrill. Riders climb six stories before hurling through two vertical loops, exceeding speeds of 40 mph.

Touring Tips   This one's short and doesn't have the large capacity of Kumba and Montu. Save it for the afternoon, when lines should be shorter.

Kiddie Rides

What It Is: Pint-sized carnival rides

Scope & Scale: Minor attractions

When to Go: Anytime

Author's Rating: Good diversion for children; ★★½

Overall Appeal by Age Group:

Pre-School	Grade School	Teens	Young Adults	Over 30	Senior Citizens
★★★	†	†	†	†	†

†Not designed for older kids and adults.

Description & Comments   These attractions are similar to the kiddie rides in Timbuktu.

Touring Tips   These rides are strategically placed near the adult attractions in this area (Kumba and Python), so one parent can keep the kids occupied while another rides.

STANLEYVILLE

Tidal Wave

What It Is: Quick, "super" water flume ride

Scope & Scale: Headliner

When to Go: Before 11 a.m. or after 3 p.m.

Special Comments: Riders must be at least 48 inches tall; you
   will get soaked

Author's Rating: A long wait for an extremely short thrill; ★★★

Overall Appeal by Age Group:

Pre-School	Grade School	Teens	Young Adults	Over 30	Senior Citizens
†	★★★	★★★	★★★	★★★	★★

†Preschoolers are generally too short to ride.

Duration of Ride: 2 minutes

Description & Comments   The Tidal Wave was king before the Orlando parks decided that a super flume should entertain you as well as get you wet. Consequently, this super water flume ride pales in comparison with Splash Mountain at Disney World or Jurassic Park at Islands of Adventure. It does do a spectacular job of getting you soaked, however. Riders board a 25-passenger boat and slowly float past stilt houses before making the climb to the top of a steep drop. The cars are designed to throw the water onto the passengers, creating a soggy experience.

Touring Tips If you didn't get enough water on the ride, stand on the bridge crossing the splash pool. An enormous wall of water shoots from each dropping car, drenching onlookers. There's also a glass wall in the area that blocks the water, but still provides a unique visual.

As you exit the attraction, or if you choose not to ride, visit Orchid Canyon. This gorgeous area features many different varieties of orchids growing around waterfalls in artificial rocks.

Stanley Falls

What It Is: Water flume ride

Scope & Scale: Major attraction

When to Go: After 3 p.m.

Special Comments: Children not accompanied by an adult must be at least 46 inches tall

Author's Rating: Basic when compared to Splash Mountain, but fun; ★★½

Overall Appeal by Age Group:

Pre-School	Grade School	Teens	Young Adults	Over 30	Senior Citizens
★★★	★★★	★★½	★★½	★★½	★★½

Duration of Ride: Approximately 3½ minutes

Description & Comments Logs drift along a winding flume before plummeting down a 40-foot drop.

Touring Tips This ride is exciting without being scary or jarring, and it is recommended for all ages. Save for the afternoon during peak season, when lines will be longer.

Stanleyville Theater/Stars of the Future

What It Is: Variety show with pint-size performers

Scope & Scale: Minor attraction

When to Go: Check daily entertainment schedule

Author's Rating: Performers' ages make this show unique; ★★★
Overall Appeal by Age Group:

Pre-School	Grade School	Teens	Young Adults	Over 30	Senior Citizens
★★½	★★½	★★½	★★★	★★★	★★★½

Duration of Show: 30 minutes

Description & Comments This variety show features young performers from around the world. Acts include a high-energy juggler, tumblers, and an aerial circus performer. Performances may vary as some of the stars have limited stays.

Touring Tips The theater's proximity to Python, Kumba, and the water attractions make seeing this show a perfect diversion for those not seeking thrills or a drenching as they wait for other members of their party.

Lory Landing

What It Is: Interactive aviary
Scope & Scale: Major attraction
When to Go: Birds are hungrier in the morning
Author's Rating: Nice; ★★★
Overall Appeal by Age Group:

Pre-School	Grade School	Teens	Young Adults	Over 30	Senior Citizens
★★★	★★★	★★★	★★★	★★★	★★★½

Description & Comments Many area attractions feature aviaries, but this is by far the biggest and the best. Tropical birds from around the world dot the lush landscape, fill the air in free flight, and are displayed in habitats. Purchase a nectar cup for $1, and some of these delightful creatures will be eating right out of your hands. The illustrated journal of a ficticious explorer helps differentiate between the many species, including lorikeets, hornbills, parrots, and avocets.

Touring Tips Try to visit before lunch because birds usually get their fill of nectar by early afternoon.

Land of the Dragons

What It Is: Kids' play area
Scope & Scale: Headliner

When to Go: Anytime

Special Comments: Only those under 56 inches can ride attractions in this area

Author's Rating: Great theming, the best of its kind in the area; ★★★★

Overall Appeal by Age Group:

Pre-School	Grade School	Teens	Young Adults	Over 30	Senior Citizens
★★★★	★★★	★★	★★	★★	★★

Description & Comments   With thrill rides galore, Busch Gardens may not seem like a place to bring little ones. This enchanting area, however, is almost reason enough for families with youngsters to visit Busch Gardens. The dragon theme is carried throughout area, creating some particularly cute attractions, including a mini–Ferris wheel with dragon egg–shaped seats and a tiny dragon water flume. Kids can climb and crawl through a huge net play area and get soaked in a fountain playground. There's also a live show featuring Dumphrey the Dragon (check daily entertainment schedule for times).

Touring Tips   This area is right next to Gwazi and on the same side of the park as Kumba, Python, and Scorpion. Those members of your group who don't do coasters can stay with the kids while others ride.

BIRD GARDENS

Gwazi

What It Is: Double wooden roller coaster

Scope & Scale: Super headliner

When to Go: Before 10 a.m. or after 3 p.m.

Special Comments: Riders must be at least 48 inches tall

Author's Rating: Thrilling; ★★★★

Overall Appeal by Age Group:

Pre-School	Grade School	Teens	Young Adults	Over 30	Senior Citizens
†	★★★★	★★★★	★★★★	★★★★	★★

†Preschoolers are generally too short to ride.

Duration of Ride: 2½ minutes

Description & Comments   Those who have a nostalgic love for wooden roller coasters will be pleased with Gwazi. And those who are fans of steel roller coasters shouldn't be disappointed with the 1.25 million feet of lumber either. For a wooden ride, this coaster delivers thrills typically associated with its steel cousins. It is actually two roller coasters in one. There are two completely different tracks—the Gwazi lion and the Gwazi tiger—intertwined to create a frenzied race, including six "flyby" encounters, in which riders pass within feet of each other.

Touring Tips   Because this is Busch Gardens' newest thrill, we suggest heading here first thing in the morning to avoid long waits. But if you have time, try the coaster again before leaving the park, as it takes on a new feel after dark.

While the two tracks offer similarly thrilling trips, the tiger side is our favorite. Queue up for both coasters in the same place and watch for an area with a huge wooden cutout of a lion and tiger. At that point, veer to the right for the tiger, left for the lion.

Adults waiting for their party to ride can visit the nearby Hospitality House for free samples of Anheuser-Busch beers. For little ones who don't ride, Land of the Dragons is also nearby.

Bird Show Theater/*For the Birds*

What It Is: Show featuring exotic birds and birds of prey
Scope & Scale: Minor attraction
When to Go: Check daily entertainment schedule
Author's Rating: Beautiful birds, but a painfully corny show; ★★
Overall Appeal by Age Group:

Pre-School	Grade School	Teens	Young Adults	Over 30	Senior Citizens
★★	★★	★	★★	★★	★★★

Duration of Show: 30 minutes

Description & Comments   With a title like *For the Birds,* we understand the show is supposed to be corny, but the bad script and even worse acting make it difficult to enjoy. Nevertheless, many of the birds are beautiful, and the owls and hawks are stunning. The grand finale features a striking bald eagle.

Touring Tips   If you're over age 21, grab a free beer at the Anheuser-Busch Hospitality House next door and head to this performance.

Even if the show's humor is a little much, seeing the beautiful birds is better than wasting time sitting at the Hospitality Center.

DINING

Busch Gardens offers a similar selection of food as sister park Sea-World. Fast food should cost about $5–6 per person, including drinks. Carved deli sandwiches on freshly baked bread are a favorite at Zagora Café. For a hot meal, try pizza or a delicious roast beef and gravy sandwich at Provisions and Terrace in Crown Colony. Stanleyville Smokehouse offers slow-smoked chicken and ribs for $5–7.

For a real treat, try a sit-down meal at Crown Colony House restaurant, which offers amazing views of the Serengeti Plain. The menu features salads, sandwiches, pasta, and seafood. For the best deal, go for the family-style dinner of fried chicken or fish with a vast selection of side dishes for $9 for adults, $4 for kids age 12 and under.

The Festhaus in Timbuktu offers great food, but could almost be considered an attraction because of its grandeur, detail, and authenticity, as well as some great entertainment. The air-conditioned, 1,000-seat restaurant instantly transports you from a Florida theme park to a magnificent German beer garden. Bare wooden tables surround a tiered stage from which dancers and a noisy, talented band perform a show of international favorites as well as lead toasts (check daily entertainment schedule for performance times). German specialties such as knockwurst, bratwurst, sauerkraut, and German potato salad are offered, along with delicious pastries and deli sandwiches. Keeping in mind that the Festhaus serves cafeteria-style and feeds thousands daily, the food is pretty good, and the prices are reasonable, with sandwiches for $5–6, desserts for $2, and beer for about $3.

For those traveling on a budget, McDonald's is within walking distance of the main entrance. Just remember to save your admission ticket and have your hand stamped as you exit.

SHOPPING

There's plenty of Busch Gardens logo merchandise, but visitors looking for something more should be happy with the vast selection. Find nature-themed gifts, such as wind chimes and jewelry, at Nature's Kingdom. African gifts and crafts, including clothing, brass urns, and leather goods, can be found throughout the park. Most have reasonable prices, although some larger, intricate items can be more expensive. For that hard-to-shop-for adult, try the West African Trading Company, Ltd., which features hand-crafted items from many countries, as well as a walk-in cigar humidor or the Anheuser-Busch Label Stable. Similar to SeaWorld, Busch Gardens offers a vast array of kid-pleasing stuffed animals, parents should be happy with the cheap prices.

Part Two

Cypress Gardens

After visiting the Central Florida megaparks, Cypress Gardens offers a laid-back day, literally allowing you time to smell the flowers. Much of what the park offers is unique and entertaining. Another refreshing change—food and souvenir prices are lower than most in the area. The park's limited number of attractions and steep price, however, might not deliver the same entertainment value as other experiences outlined in this book, such as Universal Florida and SeaWorld. (One exception might be for families with children five-years-old and younger; the kids get in free. At most other parks, it is only children under age three who get in free.)

Walt Disney World offers a beautiful array of gardens and landscape. However, avid garden lovers who rushed from attraction to attraction at the mouse house will definitely enjoy the lush landscape at the laid-back Cypress Gardens. For added "flower power," plan a visit during the Spring Flower Festival (usually mid-March through mid-May). The festival showcases several enormous floral topiary, which are larger than life and extremely charming, such as a colossal lady bug with moving antennas.

This 200-acre park is a bit more than gardens, however. It offers plenty of entertainment for young children, including Carousel Cove, a special kids area. (Older kids and teens looking for exciting attractions might find a day at Cypress Gardens boring.) Entertaining shows and animal exhibits, a unique ride that offers amazing views, and a vast array of shops round out the experience. We must point out that animal attractions should not be a main reason for visiting Cypress Gardens. The barren displays

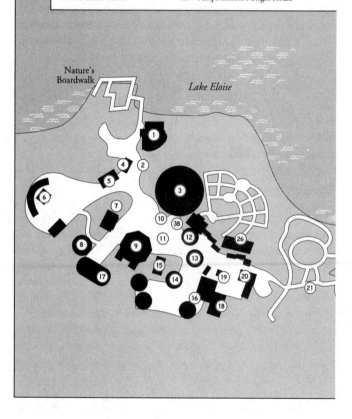

1. Birdwalk Aviary
2. Florida Historical Railway Garden
3. Island in the Sky
4. Nature's Way Refreshments
5. Antique Radio Museum
6. Nature's Arena
7. Cypress Roots
8. Crossroads Arena
9. Village Fare Food Court
10. Ice Cream Parlor
11. Cypress Junction Refreshments
12. Plantation Emporium/ My Gallery II
13. Gazebo Entertainer
14. Cypress BBQ
15. Cypress Junction
16. Carousel Cove
17. Crossroads Pavilion
18. The Palace
19. Tampa Electric's Bright House

Nature's Boardwalk

Lake Eloise

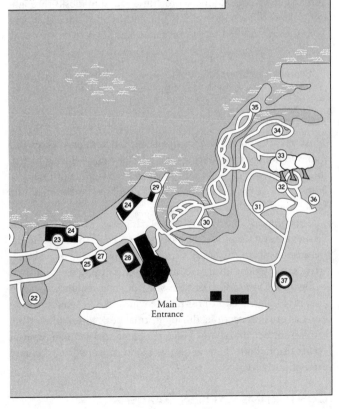

Cypress Gardens

Main
Entrance

39

found here simply cannot compete with the lush surroundings at other parks and zoos, such as Disney's Animal Kingdom.

GETTING THERE

Cypress Gardens is roughly 35 miles and a 45-minute drive from Walt Disney World. From Disney, take I-4 west to US 27 south. Turn left on FL 540, toward Winter Haven. The entrance to Cypress Gardens will be on your left. Parking is free.

ADMISSION PRICES

Following are the full-price ticket fees at press time. Coupons are available in Cypress Gardens brochures found in kiosks through-out Orlando. Discounts can also be found on the Cypress Gardens Web site and at guest services at many area hotels.

Adults: $31.95 + tax
Seniors (age 55+): $27.15
Children (ages 6–17): $14.95

ARRIVING

Most days, Cypress Gardens opens at 9:30 a.m. and closes at 5 p.m. On holidays and during two lights festivals—Spring Lights, usually February through mid-May, and the Garden of Lights & Poinsettia Festival, usually the week of Thanksgiving through early January—the park stays open later.

Spending an entire day is a relaxing way to enjoy Cypress Gardens, but if necessary, the park can be seen in about five hours. Because exploring Cypress Gardens involves a lot of walking, arrive early to take advantage of the lower morning temperatures.

Because Cypress Gardens has few rides that require waiting in line, it is a logical choice for people who'd like to avoid the long waits at other attractions during normal peak times, like spring break, summer, and major holidays. There also are many special events throughout the year and weekend concerts from January through early May.

CONTACTING CYPRESS GARDENS

For more information and a full schedule of special events, contact Cypress Gardens at (800) 282-2123. Cypress Gardens also has a fairly comprehensive Web site at www.cypressgardens.com.

Attractions

Ski Stadiums/*Ski Xtreme*

What It Is: Stunt-filled water-ski show

Scope & Scale: Super headliner

When to Go: At the beginning of your day, depending on show schedule

Author's Rating: Incredible feats, Cypress Gardens classic;

★★★★

Overall Appeal by Age Group:

Pre-school	Grade School	Teens	Young Adults	Over 30	Senior Citizens
★★★★	★★★★	★★★½	★★★★	★★★★	★★★½

Duration of Show: 30 minutes

Description & Comments Cypress Gardens has been called the "water ski capital of the world," with more than 60 years of legendary performances. *Ski Xtreme,* a 30-minute show at the stadium surrounding a bay of Lake Eloise, carries on the Cypress Gardens skiing tradition with a combination of hip music and exciting stunts. Ramp flips with multiple skiers, barefoot acts, a four-tiered human pyramid, and awe-inspiring wakeboard tricks leave the audience gasping.

One highlight occurs midway through the show, when a performer flies above the lake on a kite towed by a speed boat. At first glance, this seems similar to an uneventful parasailing display, but then the man on the kite releases the line to the boat and floats free. He zigzags through the air before landing right on target on one of the stages in front of the stadium.

For pure excitement and entertainment, the show has a rival in the SeaWorld water-ski show. However, Cypress Gardens has a greater variety of acts, including couples who perform lifts and turns while balancing on their skis.

Touring Tips A good plan for seeing Cypress Gardens is to check the ski show schedule, then plan other sight-seeing around that. Ski shows are at least an hour and 45 minutes apart, so if you miss one, it's a long wait for the next.

From the main entrance, the ski-show area is straight ahead. Two seating areas with bleachers surround a grass field directly in front of the water "stage." On cooler days, sitting on the grass will allow impatient children room to play, although the show should keep them enthralled. A spot in front will allow the best view of the entertainers as they glide onto ramps at the bottom of the bleachers or onto the shallow beach in front of the grass following their acts.

The Palace/Hot Noveau Ice

What It Is: Ice-skating performance

Scope & Scale: Headliner

When to Go: Before or after *Ski Xtreme*

Author's Rating: Entertaining, but somewhat dated; ★★½

Overall Appeal by Age Group:

Pre-school	Grade School	Teens	Young Adults	Over 30	Senior Citizens
★★½	★★½	★	★★½	★★★	★★★

Duration of Show: 25 minutes

Description & Comments   This ice-skating show includes a trip around the world, a tribute to Broadway, and a rousing patriotic finale. Taking the small stage into consideration, the talented cast performs beautiful and remarkable elements. Though the show is enjoyable, the sound system, lighting, and costumes are in need of an update. In addition, the show can't even begin to compete with the ice-skating show at Busch Gardens. The Hollywood theme of the Busch Gardens show is much more enjoyable and the choreography, costumes, and performers are several notches above those at Cypress Gardens.

Touring Tips   The entertainment schedule allows back-to-back viewing of *Ski Xtreme* and *Hot Noveau Ice.* In addition, The Palace is not terribly far from the Ski Stadiums, and the walk will take you past a beautiful Mediterranean waterfall and lush landscapes.

Plantation Gardens

What It Is: Traditional Southern garden

Scope & Scale: Minor attraction

When to Go: Anytime

Author's Rating: Lovely; ★★★

Overall Appeal by Age Group:

Pre-school	Grade School	Teens	Young Adults	Over 30	Senior Citizens
★	★	★	★★½	★★★	★★★

Description & Comments This beautiful Southern garden, with white trellises and plenty of benches (perfect for an afternoon nap, as we witnessed during a visit), features four separate areas: a butterfly garden composed of plants that attract the winged creatures; an herb garden; a vegetable garden highlighted by the purplish-green, ruffled leaves of kale; and a spectacular rose garden. The area sits along Lake Eloise, offering a gorgeous view of the sparkling waters.

Touring Tips If you'd like to duplicate elements of the gardens in your backyard, you'll need to track down a Cypress Gardens employee; many plants are not identified.

Wings of Wonder

What It Is: A greenhouse filled with butterflies

Scope & Scale: Major attraction

When to Go: Avoid visiting immediately following a *Hot Noveau Ice* show

Author's Rating: Incredibly beautiful; ★★★

Overall Appeal by Age Group:

Pre-school	Grade School	Teens	Young Adults	Over 30	Senior Citizens
★★★★	★★★★	★★★	★★★	★★★	★★★

Description & Comments More than 1,000 butterflies float through a Victorian-style greenhouse filled with plants. Touching the butterflies is discouraged, but seeing the air filled with their graceful flight is fascinating. Glass boxes near the end of the tour display butterflies in various stages of metamorphosis.

Touring Tips Although you pass the entrance to the greenhouse on the way to Plantation Gardens, visit Wings of Wonder after the gardens, as the experience exits onto the main park walkway, which would require backtracking to the gardens afterward.

Crossroads Arena/*Make 'Em Laugh*

What It Is: Circus-style show

Scope & Scale: Major attraction

When to Go: Check the daily show schedule
Author's Rating: Entertaining and funny; ★★★
Overall Appeal by Age Group:

Pre-school	Grade School	Teens	Young Adults	Over 30	Senior Citizens
★★★	★★★	★★	★★★	★★★	★★★

Duration of Show: 25 minutes

Description & Comments   The clowns steal the show in *Make 'Em Laugh,* a circus-style production that includes performers from the Moscow Circus. Dancers, an acrobatic father/daughter balancing duo, and trained dogs and cats provide other highlights.

Touring Tips   Though it might not be as polished as some Disney shows, it is fun. Kids will have a blast.

Crossroads Pavilion/Crossroads Gazebo

What They Are: Music venues
Scope & Scale: Minor attractions (Crossroads Pavilion could be considered a major attraction, depending on popularity of special guests)
When to Go: Check the daily entertainment schedule
Author's Rating: Fun, provides a break from touring; ★★½
Overall Appeal by Age Group:

Pre-school	Grade School	Teens	Young Adults	Over 30	Senior Citizens
★	★	★	★★½	★★★½	★★★½

Description & Comments   Crossroads Pavilion is home to a weekend concert series during spring months. Recent acts include the Glenn Miller Orchestra and The Lettermen. Contact Cypress Gardens or visit their Web site for more details on performers.

The Crossroads Gazebo, in the center of the main walkway, features a live band playing jazz tunes.

Touring Tips   Put on your dancin' shoes. Guests are encouraged to dance in a small area surrounding the Gazebo, and at least 20 couples were cutting a rug to their favorite tunes during one visit.

Island in the Sky

What It Is: Scenic aerial ride

Scope & Scale: Major attraction

When to Go: In the afternoon or during sunset when the park is open later

Special Comments: Could bother those with a fear of heights

Author's Rating: Excellent view; ★★★

Overall Appeal by Age Group:

Pre-school	Grade School	Teens	Young Adults	Over 30	Senior Citizens
★★★	★★★	★★½	★★★	★★★	★★★

Duration of Ride: 5 minutes

Loading Speed: Slow

Description & Comments Cypress Gardens boasts that this unique ride was the first of its kind and is one of only three in the world. A circular platform slowly rises nearly 16 stories high to offer spectacular views of Cypress Gardens and Lake Eloise. An employee points out interesting sights including Bok Tower, a historic bell tower that sits at Florida's highest elevation (295 feet).

Touring Tips Seating is single-file around a mountain painted to resemble an ash-covered volcano. There's plenty of room to leave the kids in the stroller and bring them along. Those afraid of heights might not care for this attraction, but it is by no means a thrill ride.

Nature's Way

What It Is: Animal display area

Scope & Scale: Minor attraction

When to Go: Anytime

Author's Rating: Animals are not active; ★★

Overall Appeal by Age Group:

Pre-school	Grade School	Teens	Young Adults	Over 30	Senior Citizens
★★★	★★★	★★	★★	★★	★★

Description & Comments Moss-covered trees shade this far south end of the park. Several small exhibits and habitats house animals, including alligators, snapping turtles, wallabies, and wild turkeys. The area also offers two separate animal attractions:

Nature's Boardwalk A wooden-plank boardwalk, suspended over the shores of Lake Eloise, offers a wonderful view of the water. Along the boardwalk, visitors will see deer, ducks, game fowl, and Patagonian cavies, a South American rodent.

Boardwalk Aviary A small cup of nectar can be purchased for a $1 in this interactive bird aviary. Affectionate lorys and lorikeets will swoop down onto an extended arm to take a sip of the nectar. The aviary also features tiny Muntjac deer.

Touring Tips Benches under shade trees provide a relaxing break from the heat. If you're in a hurry, or if you've visited Disney's Animal Kingdom and seen plenty of interesting creatures in naturalistic environments, skip this barren area entirely.

Nature's Arena/*Raptors & Reptiles*

What It Is: Animal show

Scope & Scale: Major attraction

When to Go: Check daily entertainment schedule

Special Comments: Not for those with a fear of snakes, could frighten small children

Author's Rating: Amusing and informative; ★★★

Overall Appeal by Age Group:

Pre-school	Grade School	Teens	Young Adults	Over 30	Senior Citizens
★★★	★★★½	★★★½	★★★	★★★	★★★

Description & Comments This small open-air stadium within Nature's Way features *Raptors & Reptiles,* an entertaining and informative performance showcasing snakes, lizards, alligators, and predatory birds. A 15-foot albino python named Banana Boy is the star of a cast including Gila monsters, rhinoceros iguanas, diamondback rattlesnakes, owls, and falcons. Presenters share interesting facts about the animals.

Touring Tips Presenters bring the animals forward for a closer look, so be prepared to either take some close-up photos or comfort kids (and reptile-phobic adults, like a few in our group) who might be alarmed by the proximity of the animals.

Florida Historical Railway Garden

What It Is: Garden featuring a model train

Scope & Scale: Diversion

When to Go: Anytime

Author's Rating: ★★

Overall Appeal by Age Group:

Pre-school	Grade School	Teens	Young Adults	Over 30	Senior Citizens
★★★	★★½	★½	★★	★★	★★★

Description & Comments This nice detour from a stroll through Nature's Way features a model train on 5,000 feet of tiny tracks. The railroad winds through lush landscape and passes small-scale models of historic Florida buildings.

Touring Tips Look closely at the small structures. They're made of unique natural materials, such as leaves and acorns.

Antique Radio Museum

What It Is: Exhibit

Scope & Scale: Diversion

When to Go: Anytime

Author's Rating: ★½

Overall Appeal by Age Group:

Pre-school	Grade School	Teens	Young Adults	Over 30	Senior Citizens
½	★	½	★	★½	★★

Description & Comments This display of old radios and radio components gives a nostalgic look at an era before television, computers, and compact discs.

Touring Tips Electronic history buffs will be entertained. Others might rather spend more time in the gardens or with the animals.

Cypress Root

What It Is: Museum

Scope & Scale: Minor attraction

When to Go: Anytime

Overall Appeal by Age Group:
Author's Rating: Nostalgic; ★★½

Pre-school	Grade School	Teens	Young Adults	Over 30	Senior Citizens
★	★	★	★★½	★★½	★★★

Description & Comments   Get a glimpse of Cypress Gardens history in this small, yet interesting exhibit. Memorabilia from the park, considered to be Florida's first, surrounds a vintage television playing reels from movies and television shows. Photos and newspaper clips give a wonderful glimpse of the original Cypress Gardens water-ski show.

Touring Tips   Part of Cypress Gardens' charm is its history, so don't miss this appealing attraction.

Cypress Junction

What It Is: Model train exhibit
Scope & Scale: Minor attraction
When to Go: Anytime
Author's Rating: Interesting; ★★½
Overall Appeal by Age Group:

Pre-school	Grade School	Teens	Young Adults	Over 30	Senior Citizens
★★★	★★½	★	★★½	★★½	★★★

Description & Comments   Twenty high-speed model trains travel on 1,100 feet of track past tiny replicas of U.S. cities and landmarks, including Miami, New Orleans, and Mount Rushmore.

Touring Tips   Billed as "the nation's most elaborate model railroad exhibit," this display is a must, especially for model-train fans.

Carousel Cove

What It Is: Children's area
Scope & Scale: Minor attraction
When to Go: Anytime the kids get restless
Author's Rating: Great for the kids and restful for parents; ★★★

Overall Appeal by Age Group:

Pre-school	Grade School	Teens	Young Adults	Over 30	Senior Citizens
★★★★	★★★★	★	★	★	★

†Only the tiniest tots can fit on these attractions. Because it keeps kids occupied, its appeal to parents and grandparents cannot be understated.

Description & Comments   This area tucked off the main walkway is perfect for children under age eight or nine. Carousel Cove features pint-sized versions of rides seen at other theme parks, including a parachute drop and carousel. A miniature golf course spans the right side of the area and can be played for an extra fee.

Touring Tips   Though miniature golf is a bargain at $2, it pales in comparison to the extremely ornate versions found around Orlando.

Botanical Gardens

What It Is: Gardens

Scope & Scale: Major attraction

When to Go: In the morning, when it's cooler, or late afternoon

Author's Rating: Gorgeous, the reason for visiting Cypress Gardens; ★★★½

Overall Appeal by Age Group:

Pre-school	Grade School	Teens	Young Adults	Over 30	Senior Citizens
★	★★	★★	★★★½	★★★★	★★★★

Description & Comments   More than 8,000 plants, trees, and blooms cover 16 acres of botanical gardens at the north end of Cypress Gardens. The entrance path offers great views of Lake Eloise, and the stately cypress trees standing guard at the shore. Along the path, several separate areas flow together to create the botanical gardens:

Florida Pool This swimming pool shaped like the Sunshine State was featured in the 1953 Esther Williams film, *Easy to Love.*

Oriental Garden An immense golden Buddha watches over this serene garden of bamboo and greenery. If you're ready for a relaxing break, take a shady seat in the Japanese tea house.

Banyan Tree Though technically part of the Oriental Gardens, this massive tree deserves a mention all to itself. Towering above the garden and stretching several feet to circle the walkway, the tree is an impressive sight. In addition, an aerial root system creates an enchanting canopy over the path.

Biblical Gardens Many of the plants mentioned in the Bible are displayed in this lush garden, including lettuce, cucumber, melon, onion, garlic, and herbs.

French Garden A symmetrical garden of blooms and foliage surrounds a sunken brick oval in this elegant area. There are also excellent views of a nearby waterfall.

Gazebo This charming white structure is the site of more than 300 weddings a year. It also offers a beautiful view of the lush green lawn, flanked by blooming trees, that leads to the Big Lagoon. The Lagoon features a fountain added to commemorate the 60th Anniversary of Cypress Gardens.

Touring Tips If you're a horticulture fanatic, make sure to allow an hour or more to explore these beautiful gardens and head there during the cooler morning hours. Others should plan for no less than a 30-minute stroll, which could be a relaxing end to the day.

Have your camera handy at the Gazebo for a unique way to document your day—a self portrait made easy by setting the timer on your camera and resting it on a platform to capture your image in a large mirror. The Gazebo will be in the background and "Cypress Gardens" will be "magically" printed at the bottom.

Botanical Boat Cruise

What It Is: Scenic boat ride

Scope & Scale: Major attraction

When to Go: Not immediately following a *Ski Xtreme* show

Special Comments: Climbing into and out of the boats can be difficult for those with physical ailments

Author's Rating: Relaxing and enjoyable; ★★★½

Overall Appeal by Age Group:

Pre-school	Grade School	Teens	Young Adults	Over 30	Senior Citizens
★★★	★★★	★★★	★★★½	★★★½	★★★½

Duration of Ride: 15 minutes

Loading Speed: Slow

Description & Comments Motor boats seating 18 passengers glide past large cypress trees with the expanse of Lake Eloise in the distance before entering a winding canal. Though the tour guide's memorized spiel is interesting, it doesn't allow the opportunity for spontaneous questions and information. Sitting near the driver at the rear of the boat allows some casual chatting, but visitors are not necessarily allowed to choose where they sit.

Touring Tips The usually short wait for this 15-minute guided water tour of the botanical gardens is definitely worth it. Though the boat ride is quick and relaxing, it should not be considered a replacement of a stroll through the gardens, which offers a closer, more complete look and some incredible photo opportunities.

Southern Breeze

What It Is: Scenic paddle-boat ride

Scope & Scale: Major attraction

When to Go: Excursions throughout day, including special brunch and dinner cruises (see the dining section below for more information)

Special Comments: Costs $4 for a regular excursion, more for meal-time trips

Author's Rating: Relaxing; ★★★

Overall Appeal by Age Group:

Pre-school	Grade School	Teens	Young Adults	Over 30	Senior Citizens
★★★	★★★½	★★★	★★★	★★★½	★★★

Description & Comments This authentic paddle boat provides a relaxing and educational view of Lake Eloise. Keep your eyes peeled for birds, including graceful herons and ospreys. Cypress Gardens claims the lake is also home to more than 200 alligators, which are more active during the spring mating season.

Touring Tips We feel an excursion should be included with the admission price, but if you're ready for a break from walking and don't mind forking over $4 per person, board *Southern Breeze*.

SHOPPING

In addition to the typical theme park shops (offering camera supplies, Cypress Gardens merchandise, candy, and resort wear), Cypress Gardens has a few unique shopping experiences.

Magnolia Mansion contains a boutique that could almost be considered an attraction—the world's largest retail selection of *Gone with the Wind* collectibles. Owner J. Faye Bell also displays vintage memorabilia from her private collection. (Bell has a one-year contract with Cypress Gardens that may or may not be extended in November 1999, look up www.gwtwmemories.com for more information.)

An icon of Dixie, Southern belles are the ambassadors of Cypress Gardens. Demure in their ruffled dresses, these ladies can be seen meandering through the park. For a little added fun or for special occasions, the Junior Belle Boutique will transform young girls into Southern belles. For $39.95, girls receive a brief training session, makeup, hair styling, and a long, billowing dress to wear in the park for two to three hours.

Gardening, Etc. and Butterfly Shop might be of interest to gardeners. Find bulbs, seeds, books, toys, T-shirts, and so on.

Many of the shops don't open until midmorning or early afternoon, so save shopping until the end of your day.

DINING

Cypress Gardens' food prices are lower than at most theme parks. Typical fare (popcorn, soft pretzels, funnel cakes, ice cream sodas) can be found throughout the park for around $2 or less. Baker's Dozen offers fresh-baked fruit Danishes, muffins, orange or grapefruit juice, and coffee for breakfast or a snack.

For something more substantial but in the fast-food range, try Cypress BBQ, featuring smoked meats ($6 or so) and yummy desserts (under $3), or Village Fare Food Court, serving deli sandwiches, burgers, salads, fried or baked chicken, and roast beef dinners (around $7 per person).

Crossroads Restaurant & Terrace offers good full-service fare at moderate prices. On cooler, rain-free days, the shaded outdoor terrace is the perfect location for lunch or dessert. Choose from sandwiches, salads, and entrees, including pasta, quiche, and chicken puff pastry. Main course prices range from $6 to $8. For just a few dollars more don't miss dessert. The Key lime and pecan pies are excellent.

For an interesting meal, combine a trip on the *Southern Breeze* with dinner or brunch (offered only on Sunday). For $15.95 for adults, $9.95 for children, cruise around Lake Eloise dining on a Sunday brunch buffet of salads, cheeses, breads, roast turkey and ham, vegetables, and desserts. From Sunday to Thursday, a dinner trip features a buffet including prime rib, grilled salmon, salads, vegetables, and dessert at a cost of $17.95 for adults, $10.95 for children. Dinner on Friday or Saturday is full-service with your choice of prime rib, veal, or salmon for $19.95 for adults, $11.95 for children. Excursion times vary.

Part Three

Gatorland

There's something simply fascinating about Gatorland. Maybe it's the apparent "grittiness" of the park, billed as the "alligator capital of the world." Perhaps it's the fact that Gatorland is far from politically correct in the extremely sanitary city of Orlando. Maybe it's just the outright coolness of these creatures, which strike as much interest in people as they do fear. Whatever it is, for the right kind of person, this park is not to be missed.

For more than 50 years, Gatorland has existed as a roadside wonder. Before the days of magic castles and studio backlots, visitors flocked to the Sunshine State for its beaches and wildlife. Sprinkled along the highways that linked the state's natural attractions were tiny outposts of tourism—"must-see" roadside stops meant to break up the monotony of travel. Gatorland fell brilliantly into this category. The park was ripe with tourist appeal— who can resist a park that hawks Florida's most infamous resident, the alligator?

Today, Gatorland seems to disappear in the clutter of touristy Orlando. It doesn't try to be one of the high-falutin' theme parks in its backyard. Although the attraction has grown to more than 100 acres, it still rightfully trumpets its manageability as "Florida's best half-day attraction." Of course compared to Walt Disney World, it is pretty modest in its presentation, but only as much as a park with a few thousand alligators can be. In short, the park celebrates the spirit of "true Florida." For those who want variety in their sight-seeing itinerary, minus Mickey Mouse and miles of sandy beaches, Gatorland is willing to take the challenge.

GETTING THERE

From Disney, take FL 192 (or the Osceola Parkway, if you don't mind paying a few bucks in tolls) to FL 441 (Orange Blossom Trail). Turn left. Gatorland is on your right.

From Orlando, take I-4 to FL 528 (Beeline Highway). Exit at Consulate and turn right. Make a right on FL 441 (Orange Blossom Trail). Gatorland is approximately seven miles south, between the Osceola Parkway and FL 417 (the Central Florida Greeneway). Parking is free.

ADMISSION PRICES

Following are the full-price admission prices at press time. Coupons are available in Gatorland brochures found on kiosks throughout Orlando. The park also has AAA and AARP discounts.

Adult: $16.93 + tax
Children (ages 3–12): $7.48
Children under age 3: Free

ARRIVING

Gatorland is open daily from 9 a.m. until dusk. ("Dusk" is a relative term. Gatorland suggests 6 p.m. during the winter and 7 p.m. during the rest of the year.) Gators don't mind rain, so the attraction is open rain or shine.

Gatorland bills itself as a half-day attraction, which makes it the perfect alternative when you don't have a full day to spend at Walt Disney World, SeaWorld, or Kennedy Space Center. Plan to spend about three to four hours to see it well. However, the park lends itself to any type of schedule. With nearby parking, and the park's manageable size, it is easy to come and go.

Shows and feeding times are scheduled throughout the day, with performances shortly after opening, after lunch, and early evening. Performances are scheduled for easy back-to-back viewing.

Check the show schedule when you arrive. Because the shows are "can't-miss" attractions, plan your schedule around them. There are plenty of diversions near each show area. The *Jungle Crocs of the World* feeding "show" is the farthest away, requiring a substantial walk, so keep that in mind when heading for this area of the park.

CONTACTING GATORLAND

For more information, contact Gatorland at (800) 393-JAWS. Gatorland also has a Web site at www.gatorland.com.

Attractions

Gator Jumparoo Show

What It Is: Read the name? 'Nuff said

Scope & Scale: Super headliner

When to Go: Check entertainment schedule

Author's Rating: Yikes!; ★★★

Overall Appeal by Age Group:

Pre-school	Grade School	Teens	Young Adults	Over 30	Senior Citizens
★★★	★★★★	★★★	★★★	★★★	★★★

Duration of Show: 15 minutes

Description & Comments   Who would have ever thought that 10-foot alligators weighing hundreds of pounds could jump for dinner? There's something awe-inspiring about these animals as they leap out of the water for a dangling chicken. Don't worry—this is the store-bought variety . . . no feathers!

Touring Tips   This is a no-frills show. There isn't even seating here, so be sure to arrive at least ten minutes before show time to stake your claim along the railing.

Gatorland Train

What It Is: A circling train

Scope & Scale: Diversion

When to Go: Any time for a quick rest of your feet

Author's Rating: Can a gator highjack a train?; ★★

Overall Appeal by Age Group:

Pre-school	Grade School	Teens	Young Adults	Over 30	Senior Citizens
★★★	★★★	★	★★	★★	★★

Duration of Ride: 6 minutes

Description & Comments   The train provides a good orientation to Gatorland. If anything, go for the humorous narration provided by one of the "Florida crackers" who staff the park. Chances are, the guy who narrates your ride will turn up again later in the gator wrestling or *Jumparoo* show.

Touring Tips   Although the train does make one stop near the Wrestling Stadium, it is completely unnecessary, as it is just a short walk away.

Jungle Crocs of the World

What It Is: A rare collection of crocodiles

Scope & Scale: Super headliner

When to Go: Around feeding time

Author's Rating: Love the catchy theme song; ★★★

Overall Appeal by Age Group:

Pre-school	Grade School	Teens	Young Adults	Over 30	Senior Citizens
★★	★★★	★★★	★★★	★★★	★★★

Duration of Show: 10 minutes (feeding show)

Description & Comments   Stepping onto the boardwalk leading you to Gatorland's newest animal exhibit, you'll quickly realize that this isn't a normal attraction. Speakers lining the walkway play a song devoted entirely to Owen Godwin and his many adventures to claim this collection of "jungle crocs." The excitement builds at every turn—and every verse—until you reach the large area with the exhibits. There are four total, featuring crocodiles from America, Cuba, Asia, South America, and Africa's Nile River. This exhibit features a rare collection of crocodiles, such as the Cuban crocodile, the smallest and most dangerous of breeds that can leap from the water like a dolphin to catch birds in flight. This area includes plenty of sight gags, including downed planes and pup tents that mysteriously lack any human beings.

Touring Tips   Be sure to stick around for a feeding session, listed on the show schedule.

Gator Wrestling Stadium/*Gator Wrestlin' Show*

What It Is: Wisecracking display of courage

Scope & Scale: Super headliner

When to Go: Check entertainment schedule

Author's Rating: Not to be missed; ★★★

Overall Appeal by Age Group:

Pre-school	Grade School	Teens	Young Adults	Over 30	Senior Citizens
★★	★★★★	★★★★	★★★	★★★	★★★

Duration of Show: 15 minutes

Description & Comments   There are no bad views in the 800-seat stadium. There is one seat, however, that most audience members would rather not have. That's the perch on the back of an alligator in a sandy pit in the middle of the theater. Here, a wisecracking fool keeps the audience spellbound with his courage—and outright stupidity—for 15 minutes. The show features two "crackers," the nickname for Florida ranchers who often cracked their whips to get their animals to move. In their best Southern accents, the two play off of one another while one unfortunate soul wrestles the gator, opens its mouth, and even (gulp!) places his chin under its snout.

Touring Tips   Arrive a bit early to see the "wrestlers" warming up. Although every side offers a good view, the red bleachers typically have the best view.

Gatorland Zoo

What It Is: A collection of animal displays

Scope & Scale: Diversion

When to Go: Between shows

Author's Rating: Fun, but not as cool as gators; ★★

Overall Appeal by Age Group:

Pre-school	Grade School	Teens	Young Adults	Over 30	Senior Citizens
★★★	★★★	★★	★★	★★	★★

Description & Comments   Dozens of animal exhibits line the 150-foot main walkway, including bears, Florida white-tailed deer, emus, llamas, snakes, turtles, and birds. Allie's Barnyard petting zoo—always a favorite among young children—contains the usual collection of goats and sheep. The walk-through Very Merry Aviary is stocked with lorikeets, tiny multicolored birds that are trained to land on visitors' shoulders to drink nectar from a cup (available for $1). Those who love snakes should visit the snake pit, a collection of slithering creatures. Also, don't miss Monty the Python, a 15-foot Burmese python on display at the far north end. Camel rides (an unusual sight, to say the least) are available for $5.

Touring Tips   Zoo exhibits are near both main show areas and are perfect "filler" between other shows. Be sure to bring along a handful of quarters to buy animal food. It's a minimal cost for a big thrill.

Snakes of Florida

What It Is: An exhibit of exotic Florida snakes
Scope & Scale: Diversion
When to Go: Between shows
Author's Rating: Creepy but cool; ★★
Overall Appeal by Age Group:

Pre-school	Grade School	Teens	Young Adults	Over 30	Senior Citizens
★	★★★	★★★	★★	★★	★★

Description & Comments   A rather informative display featuring a dozen or so snakes, including king snakes and coach whip snakes. Signs that accompany the display feature a lot of good information about these slithering creatures.

Touring Tips   While waiting for the *Gator Jumparoo* show to begin, older children can check out this exhibit.

Lilly's Pad and Alligator Alley

What It Is: A wet and dry playground for kids
Scope & Scale: Major attraction
When to Go: When the temperature kicks up a notch
Author's Rating: A welcome way to cool down; ★★★
Overall Appeal by Age Group:

Pre-school	Grade School	Teens	Young Adults	Over 30	Senior Citizens
★★★	★★★★	★★★	★★★	★★	★

Description & Comments   Small children will go berserk when they see this water playground. Gatorland really shines here, with an area that rivals the children's "play fountains" at other Orlando parks. You'll find several interactive fountains and other water-soaking games. Nearby, a "dry" playground is available for those who don't want to get wet.

Touring Tips   You might want to let your children loose at Lilly's Pad earlier in the day, giving them plenty of time to dry off in the hot Florida sun.

Alligator Breeding Marsh and Bird Sanctuary

What It Is: A breeding ground for gators in a picturesque setting
Scope & Scale: Diversion
When to Go: At the warmer part of the day
Author's Rating: Gator-riffic!; ★★★
Overall Appeal by Age Group:

Pre-school	Grade School	Teens	Young Adults	Over 30	Senior Citizens
★★	★★	★★	★★★	★★★	★★★

Description & Comments   The alligator breeding marsh is one of Gatorland's most unexpected attractions. In the middle of a park of zoolike cages and enclosures, is this rather large body of water, home to nearly 200 alligators in their natural setting. Once you consider that the park also doubles as an "alligator farm," selling the meat and hides of these frightening creatures, it begins to make more sense. Whatever the outcome, it is great to stand and watch the animals doing what they do. Much of the time, this is nothing. Remember that alligators are cold-blooded creatures, so they are a bit sluggish in the cold. To see them in their full glory, you must visit during a warm time of the year or during alligator nesting in June. For different views, be sure to check out this area from each level of the three-story observation tower. The marsh is also a haven for bird-watchers. Every year, more than 4,000 birds make Gatorland home, including green, blue, and tricolored herons; cattle egret; and cormorant. At feeding time, the trees along the boardwalk marsh fill with water birds, including rare and protected species.

Touring Tips   For the best view, bring binoculars. It is truly spectacular to feed the gators here (a bag of fish is $5). There is a smaller feeding area elsewhere, but you'll get more of a show if you take the goodies here. On one visit, a family brought several loaves of bread to feed the gators. It was a fascinating sight, and it attracted what seemed like hundreds of creatures. Check the trees on your right as you walk toward the petting farm, with the marsh behind you. On a June visit, there were hundreds of nesting herons, with the accompanying chirps of their young. Because the second level is above the trees, it provides a rare look at these birds.

Swamp Walk

What It Is: Boardwalk through undisturbed nature

Scope & Scale: Diversion

When to Go: When you need some quiet time

Author's Rating: Natural Florida; ★★★

Overall Appeal by Age Group:

Pre-school	Grade School	Teens	Young Adults	Over 30	Senior Citizens
★★	★★	★	★★★	★★★	★★★★

Description & Comments   Cross the swinging bridge that leads to a boardwalk trail through a beautiful natural swamp. So far removed from the rest of the attraction that many visitors fail to discover it, the walk is easily one of the most exotic and unusual promenades to be found in all of Florida. Believe it or not, the swamp is actually part of the headwaters for the Florida Everglades, the critically important South Florida swampland hundreds of miles away. Winding gracefully with no apparent impact on the environment, the walk, flanked by towering cypress and overhung with Spanish moss, disappears deep into the lush, green swamp. Simultaneously tranquil and serene, yet bursting with life, the swamp radiates a primeval loveliness.

Touring Tips   Visit the Swamp Walk before sunset, when the mosquitoes come out to feast on unsuspecting Gatorland tourists.

SHOPPING

If you are looking for a tacky Florida souvenir for that prized spot on your mantle, Gatorland is the place. Similar to shops that line US 192, the park hawks everything gator-related that you could ever imagine—and even a few things you would never consider. There are also several merchandise carts throughout the park and two unique photo locations.

DINING

Dining at Gatorland can either be an adventure or noneventful. It's a letdown if you come to sample its regular menu items. They are nothing spectacular, but then again they are also fairly inexpensive by Orlando theme-park standards. A hamburger is $2.25 and a kids meal is $3.99. The menu is varied, however, and includes chicken breast and a "fish 'n chips" basket.

But who comes to Gatorland to eat a hot dog? No self-respecting individual can visit without trying at least a bite of gator meat. Pearl's Smokehouse features two such items, including gator nuggets and gator ribs. Although both sound quite frightening at first, so must have chicken nuggets to our ancestors. Yes, the gator nuggets do taste like chicken, but more spicy and much more tough. They come with barbecue dipping sauces to mask any unfamiliar tastes. The ribs are a bit more intimidating, but quite good. They are also quite small and, consequently, contain small bones, so be careful. Try the sampler platter, which gives you a taste of both treats.

Part Four

Kennedy Space Center

You may be old enough to remember the excitement and antici-pation of the early days of space exploration. If not, you've prob-ably seen the movies. Regardless, the pioneer spirit of the space program—sparked when President John F. Kennedy promised to land a man on the moon—is contagious.

Kennedy Space Center has been the training area and launch site for most major U.S. space programs, including Project Mercury's manned orbital missions, Project Apollo's voyages to the moon, and the Space Shuttle program. In addition, weather and communications satellites are regularly put into orbit from here.

By the end of 1999, Kennedy Space Center is slated to have completed it's $100 million expansion project. Most of the upgrad-ing and additions are already complete, but two final exhibits, The Early Space Exploration exhibit and Exploration in the New Millenium, should open in December. These attractions will be two sides of the same coin; The Early Space Exploration exhibit describing important early missions like Mercury and Gemini, and Exploration in the New Millenium, showcasing a replica of the recent Mars Viking Lander as well as pieces of the red planet.

Kennedy Space Center Visitor Complex does a wonderful job of capturing the spirit of adventure—and the uncertainty—of the early days of America's space program. It also offers an unique glimpse into the latest NASA advancements. But beware, inci-dence of "intragroup touring incompatibility" (members of the same group having strongly conflicting interests or touring ob-jectives) is high at the Space Center. Those whose hearts have been captured by the spirit of space exploration can easily busy themselves until the doors are locked at closing time. Children, at the other extreme, haven't the patience or inclination for all the reading required by the exhibits and often fizzle out after a couple of hours. The average tourist, by our reckoning, will selectively see the highlights, including the bus tour, in about four to five and a half hours. We've found that these "average tourists" then hole up in the cafeteria or souvenir shop, waiting for one or more space buffs in their party to reappear. A better option, however, is to leave space junkies at Kennedy Space Center, while the rest of the group heads to one of the nearby beaches for a little fun in the sun before meeting up at the Space Center when it closes.

GETTING THERE

Kennedy Space Center Visitor Complex is an easy day trip from most Central Florida attractions. From Orlando, visitors can take FL 528 (Beeline Highway toll road) east. (A round trip on the Beeline will cost about $5 in tolls, so have some cash handy.) Turn onto FL 407 north, then FL 405 east, and follow to the Kennedy Space Center Visitor Complex. You can also take Colonial Drive (FL 50), and travel east to Route 405, but the Beeline is definitely the quickest and easiest route. Parking is free.

ADMISSION PRICES

Several attractions are free. For the major highlights, like the bus tour and IMAX films, there are several packages to choose from. Also, if you're short on time, tickets for the tour and the movies can be purchased separately. For most, the Crew Pass is the way to go. The Mission Pass is recommended only for serious space junkies.

Crew Pass
(All paid attractions, the bus tour, and one IMAX movie)
Adults: $19
Children (ages 3–11): $15
Children under age 3: Free
Mission Pass
(Crew Pass plus an additional IMAX movie)
Adults: $26
Children (ages 3–9): $20

Bus Tour and Paid Attractions
Adults: $14
Children (ages 3–9): $10
IMAX Movies
Adults: $7.50 per movie
Children (ages 3–9): $5.50 per movie

ARRIVING

Kennedy Space Center Visitor Complex is open from 9 a.m. to "dusk," meaning anytime between 6 to 8:30 p.m., depending on the time of the year. Unlike other area attractions, the Space Center is closed on Christmas day and may close for certain shuttle launches. Call ahead before making the drive.

The Space Center is a confusing conglomeration of free and paid attractions. All visitors start off at the Visitor Complex hub, where free attractions include the Rocket Garden, Merritt Island National Wildlife Refuge Exhibit, the Children's Play Dome, the Astronaut Memorial, Mission to Mars, Gallery of Space Flight, and Shuttle Plaza.

Paid sights include several IMAX films, Robot Scouts, Universe Theater's *Quest for Life,* and a few exhibits along a bus tour, such as Apollo Saturn V Center, Launch Complex 39 Observation Gantry, and the International Space Station Center.

Each of the IMAX movies is about 40 minutes long, and the bus tour alone can take more than three hours. If this leaves you feeling overwhelmed, you're right, there's a lot of ground to cover here. The wrong approach is to race from attraction to attraction in one day. Instead, take it slow and soak in some of the better attractions, leaving the others behind.

Most visitors should start their day with some of the exhibits at the hub, which provide an informative background on space history. Then, head to the most significant part of the Kennedy Space Center Visitor Complex, the bus tour. Although a highlight of a Space Center visit, the bus tour can be frustrating for those accustomed to instant gratification. Buses come frequently (every 10 minutes), but if your timing is off, you can stand a full 15 minutes before boarding, then sit on the bus for a few minutes before taking off. All of this is followed by a 10-minute trip to each destination, but once on the bus, things do get better.

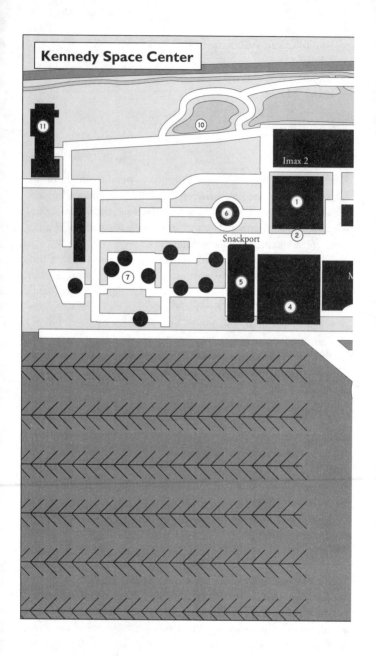

Kennedy Space Center

Imax 2

Snackport

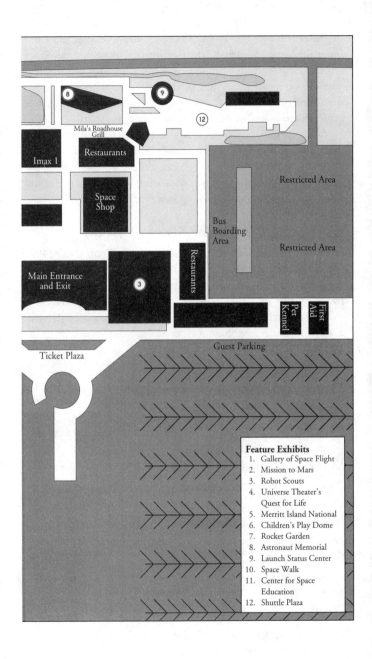

Mila's Roadhouse Grill

Restaurants

Imax 1

Space Shop

Restaurants

Main Entrance and Exit

Bus Boarding Area

Restricted Area

Restricted Area

Pet Kennel

First Aid

Ticket Plaza

Guest Parking

Feature Exhibits
1. Gallery of Space Flight
2. Mission to Mars
3. Robot Scouts
4. Universe Theater's Quest for Life
5. Merritt Island National
6. Children's Play Dome
7. Rocket Garden
8. Astronaut Memorial
9. Launch Status Center
10. Space Walk
11. Center for Space Education
12. Shuttle Plaza

Buses will take you to LC 39 Observation Gantry, and from there to Apollo Saturn V, then on to the International Space Station Center. Each of the stops involves movies and displays that are very text-heavy but interesting. The movies are wonderful and are of documentary quality, but after a while some may begin to grow tired of the movie-bus-movie-bus shuffle.

After the bus tour, see at least one of the IMAX movies. The five-and-a-half-story screens provide amazing views, and the sound systems are excellent. You can choose from exploring the weightless environment of a space station, peeking at the future in 3D, or witnessing the thrilling sensation of space flight.

CONTACTING KENNEDY SPACE CENTER

For more information about Kennedy Space Center, call (407) 452-2121. You can also try (800) KSC-INFO, but this is a quick recorded message of basic information that doesn't allow you to transfer to an actual person. You can also visit www.kscvisitor.com, which has a page just for kids. The Space Center will mail you a brochure about tours, as well as launch schedule information.

Attractions at the Hub

IMAX Films

What It Is: Large format films projected onto huge screens with incredible sound systems

Scope & Scale: Headliner

When to Go: Check daily entertainment schedule; perfect when it is raining

Author's Rating: Excellent; ★★★½

Overall Appeal by Age Group:

Pre-school	Grade School	Teens	Young Adults	Over 30	Senior Citizens
★★★	★★★★	★★	★★★	★★★½	★★★½

Duration of Shows: Approximately 40 minutes

Description & Comments   Kennedy Space Center offers three excellent IMAX films:

The Dream Is Alive Get inside the cabin with amazing in-flight footage shot by astronauts in space. You'll enjoy the beauty that astronauts experience firsthand, and learn about the challenges of living in space.

Mission to Mir Examine Russia and America's joint efforts in space while learning about life aboard the space station.

L5: First City in Space See a future space city through the eyes of a seven-year-old girl who was born on the space colony in this 3D film. Explore her world as she tends to their farm, goes to school, and lives a normal home life. Kids will enjoy the 3D effects of the film, and the idea that one day they, too, may experience a life in space.

Touring Tips If you must choose just one of these films, *The Dream Is Alive* is definitely the best. In all three, we recommend sitting toward the back of the theater for the best view and to fully experience the awesome sound system. You will need to arrive early because these theaters are fairly small.

Typical of most theaters, popcorn, candy, and sodas are available in the lobby.

Universe Theater/*Quest for Life*

What It Is: Film about life on other planets
Scope & Scale: Minor attraction
When to Go: Anytime
Author's Rating: Interesting; ★★★
Overall Appeal by Age Group:

Pre-school	Grade School	Teens	Young Adults	Over 30	Senior Citizens
★	★★★	★★★	★★	★★	★★★

Duration of Show: 15 minutes

Description & Comments Does life exist on other planets? Leading scientists lend evidence that there may have been life on Mars. The film addresses the likelihood of other planets sustaining life and NASA's plans to determine if life exists in other parts of the universe.

Touring Tips This is a good last stop before heading to the hotel.

Robot Scouts

What It Is: Walk-through exhibit featuring robots

Scope & Scale: Minor attraction

When to Go: At the end of the day, if there's time

Author's Rating: ★★

Overall Appeal by Age Group:

Pre-school	Grade School	Teens	Young Adults	Over 30	Senior Citizens
★★	★★★	★★	★★	★★	★★

Description & Comments   Robot "Starquester 2000" will take you through this exhibit of NASA's past, present, and future robotic space explorers. "Starquester 2000" interacts with other space probes like Viking Mars Lander and the Hubble Telescope, to explain how robotic space exploration aids human exploration.

Touring Tips   You can hit this exhibit on entering the Center, before the bus tours.

Astronaut Memorial

What It Is: Memorial to those who died for space exploration

Scope & Scale: Minor attraction

When to Go: At the end of the tour

Author's Rating: Touching tribute; ★★★

Overall Appeal by Age Group:

Pre-school	Grade School	Teens	Young Adults	Over 30	Senior Citizens
★	★	★	★★	★★★	★★★

Description & Comments   The entire memorial tilts and swivels to follow the sun, while mirrors direct the sun's rays onto glass names etched in a black marble slab.

Touring Tips   Visit the kiosk on the side of the Gallery Center Building. There you'll find computers that offer background information on the astronauts on the memorial.

Gallery of Space Flight

What It Is: Museum of space artifacts

Scope & Scale: Minor attraction

When to Go: At the start of your trip

Author's Rating: Neat artifacts; ★★★

Overall Appeal by Age Group:

Pre-school	Grade School	Teens	Young Adults	Over 30	Senior Citizens
½	★	★	★★½	★★★	★★★

Description & Comments This gallery will give you a good overview of space exploration. On display: the first Mercury spacecraft, a Gemini capsule, and the suit worn by Neil Armstrong on the moon.

Touring Tips This is an excellent place to start your tour.

Children's Play Dome

What It Is: Kiddie playground

Scope & Scale: Diversion

When to Go: If your older kids are looking at the Rocket Garden, supervise the young ones here

Author's Rating: ★★

Overall Appeal by Age Group:

Pre-school	Grade School	Teens	Young Adults	Over 30	Senior Citizens
★★★	★★	—	—	—	—

Description & Comments This little playground, under cover from the hot sun, is a nice diversion for kids. It is similar to the kids' areas at other attractions, but a space theme prevails.

Touring Tips One adult can take the older kids to an IMAX movie or on a stroll through the Rocket Garden, while another supervises the little ones here.

Rocket Garden

What It Is: Outdoor rocket display

Scope & Scale: Diversion

When to Go: Before you head home

Author's Rating: Unique display; ★★

Overall Appeal by Age Group:

Pre-school	Grade School	Teens	Young Adults	Over 30	Senior Citizens
★	★	★	★	★★	★★

Description & Comments   Rockets and spacecraft dot a vast lawn. The big rockets take center stage and are the perfect backdrop for group photos.

Touring Tips   Morning and afternoon guided tours are offered. Check the sign near the garden entrance for times.

Shuttle Plaza

What It Is: View a space shuttle model

Scope & Scale: Minor attraction

When to Go: Immediately before or after bus tour

Author's Rating: Impressive up close; ★★

Overall Appeal by Age Group:

Pre-school	Grade School	Teens	Young Adults	Over 30	Senior Citizens
★	★★★	★★	★★	★★	★★★

Description & Comments   This full-size replica of the space shuttle will give you a glimpse of what it's like to be an astronaut working and living in space. You'll see the flight deck, where astronauts fly the orbiter during launch and landing, and the mid-deck, where shuttle crews work on experiments, sleep, and eat.

Touring Tips   This exhibit is easy to forget if you're racing to the bus tour because it's off the beaten path. Nevertheless, there may be a long line. We suggest trying back later in the afternoon rather than waiting for this interesting, but uneventful tour.

Launch Status Center

What It Is: Live launch briefings and artifacts on display

Scope & Scale: Major attraction

When to Go: After visiting the Shuttle Plaza

Author's Rating: Informative; ★★★

Overall Appeal by Age Group:

Pre-school	Grade School	Teens	Young Adults	Over 30	Senior Citizens
★	★★	★★★	★★★	★★★	★★★★

Description & Comments   The artifacts are neat, but most enjoyable are the live briefings that take place on the hour, between

11 a.m. and 5 p.m. Space Center communicators and live footage from throughout the complex give a glimpse into what is happening at the Space Center the day of your visit.

Touring Tips Visit just days before a launch and you'll catch the real action, which could include live video from the shuttle.

Kennedy Space Center Bus Tour

Buses run every 10 minutes and make three stops around the complex. Touring is at your own pace, but the entire trip, making all the stops, should average about three and a half hours. In transit, there's no staring into "space." Television monitors show informative segments on space exploration to prepare you for the next destination. Think of this time as cramming for an exam. If possible, sit near the front of the bus, on the right side, for a better view of buildings in the area. Also, if you're lucky, an alert bus driver will point out wildlife—which included an impressive bald eagle nest on one visit—along the way to the following stops:

LC 39 Observation Gantry and Theater

What It Is: Movie and observation area that focuses on the Space Shuttle

Scope & Scale: Major attraction

When to Go: Anytime

Author's Rating: Get up close and personal with shuttle launch pads; ★★★★

Overall Appeal by Age Group:

Pre-school	Grade School	Teens	Young Adults	Over 30	Senior Citizens
★★	★★★	★★	★★★	★★★★	★★★★

Description & Comments The LC 39 exhibits celebrate the Space Shuttle—the first spacecraft designed to be reusable. A seven-minute film at the LC 39 Theater, narrated by shuttle astronaut Marsha Ivins, explains how NASA engineers and technicians service the shuttle before launch. After the film, the doors open to dump you into a room with model displays. From here, head to the observation gantry, which puts you less than one mile away from Launch Pads 39A and 39B, the only sites for launching the space shuttle. These are also the pads from which the Saturn V rockets blasted off to the moon during the Apollo program.

Touring Tips   You'll be tempted to race to the observation gantry, but watching the film first definitely gives a better appreciation of the views offered at the gantry. Once at the observation gantry, look for the Crawlerway path, a road nearly as wide as an eight-lane highway and more than three miles long. It was specially constructed to bear the weight of a Crawler-Transporter (six million pounds), which moves the Space Shuttle from the Vehicle Assembly Building to the launch pad.

Apollo Saturn V Center

What It Is: Exhibit celebrating the race to the moon

Scope & Scale: Super headliner

When to Go: Anytime

Author's Rating: Where else can you touch a moon rock?;
    ★★★★

Overall Appeal by Age Group:

Pre-school	Grade School	Teens	Young Adults	Over 30	Senior Citizens
★★★	★★★★	★★★	★★★★	★★★★	★★★★

Description & Comments   The Apollo Saturn V Center is a gigantic building (actually constructed around the rocket!) with several displays. All guests must enter a "holding area" where you'll see a nine-minute film on the race to the moon. This film is good, but things only get better.

The next stop is the Firing Room Theater, which catapults you back in time to December 1, 1968, for the launch of the first successful manned mission to the moon. Actual remnants of the original 1960s Firing Room, complete with launch consoles and countdown clocks, set the mood. Once the show is under way, three large screens take you back to that day with original footage from the Space Center. During this 10-minute presentation, you'll sense the stress of the launch commanders and feel like you're experiencing the actual launch through some fun special effects.

This is a pride-inducing presentation that prepares you for the real meat and potatoes of the Apollo/Saturn V Center—the actual 363-foot Saturn V moon rocket. When the doors of the Firing Room Theater open, guests are instantly overwhelmed by the size of the rocket. The amount of power the rocket produced on blast-off (7.5 million pounds of thrust) could light up New York City for an hour and 15 minutes. In addition, this room is filled with space artifacts, including the van used to transport astronauts to the launch pad, a lunar module, and Jim Lovell's Apollo 13 space suit. But there are more than just dusty relics here. They do a great job of telling the history of the era with story boards along the walls to document the highlights of each Apollo mission.

If you're up for another movie, visit the Lunar Theater. Neil Armstrong leads you through his lunar landing during this suspenseful documentary on Apollo 11. The 12-minute film is nearly perfect, with the exception of the lame effects at the end—a lunar module lands and a wax Armstrong pops up from the "moon."

Touring Tips If you're traveling with kids, they may well be restless by now. Check out the interactive exhibits, or maybe step outside. There is a patio near the dining area where your family can get some fresh air.

Cape Canaveral Tour

What It Is: Bus tour to Cape Canaveral

Scope & Scale: Headliner

When to Go: Check the daily schedule, it usually runs at 1 p.m.

Special Comments: Tour is frequently canceled due to launch activity

Author's Rating: A piece of NASA history; ★★★½

Overall Appeal by Age Group:

Pre-school	Grade School	Teens	Young Adults	Over 30	Senior Citizens
★★	★★½	★★½	★★★½	★★★★	★★★★

Duration of Tour: Approximately two hours

Description & Comments Situated about 15 miles from Kennedy Space Center, Cape Canaveral Air Station is an active launch facility where unmanned rockets are sent into space on NASA, military, and commercial missions. Even more interesting, though, is Cape Canaveral's place in history as the original home of the U.S. space program. It is here that the early Mercury missions, as well as the first Americans, were launched into space. And unlike the Space Center bus excursion with its far-away viewing, this tour allows you to actually explore these historical locations up close.

A highlight of the tour is the Air Force Space & Mission Museum, home of the world's largest outdoor collection of missiles on display.

Touring Tips   Unfortunately, you are not allowed to tour at your own pace and must depart with the same group on the same bus.

The International Space Station

What It Is: Observation area

Scope & Scale: Minor attraction

When to Go: Anytime; provides good cover if it rains

Author's Rating: Don't spend too much time here; ★★

Overall Appeal by Age Group:

Pre-school	Grade School	Teens	Young Adults	Over 30	Senior Citizens
★	★	★★	★★	★★	★★★

Description & Comments   Kennedy Space Center touts the International Space Station as "the most ambitious space program since the Apollo moon landings." If that's really the case, it's a shame this exhibit isn't more exciting. Your first stop is a five-minute film on the purpose and importance of the space station. After the film, you can either explore some of the full-scale mock parts or tour the actual facility NASA is using to prepare components of the real space station, scheduled to be complete in 2003.

Touring Tips   The International Space Station Center is the last stop on the bus tour. If you're running out of steam, bypass the center and head straight for the hub to catch an IMAX film.

VIEWING A LAUNCH

Does your child dream of becoming an astronaut? Maybe you remember the exact day Neil Armstrong set foot on the moon. If so, seeing a live launch is truly awe-inspiring and will leave you with a memory you'll never forget.

Kennedy Space Center offers a bus trip to a viewing site about six miles from the launch area for $10 per person. You can also purchase a ticket that includes the bus trip, a mission briefing presentation, and one IMAX film for $17.50. You might be able to make reservations up to a week in advance, but sometimes tickets are only sold on a first come, first served basis at the Ticket Pavilion located at the main entrance of the Visitor Complex. For more information, call (407) 452-2121, ext. 4400.

Launches can also be seen outside of Kennedy Space Center along U.S. Highway 1 in Titusville, Florida, and along Highway A1A in Cape Canaveral and Cocoa Beach. All of these locations can be reached from FL 528 (Beeline Highway toll road) east. You should arrive early (about three hours in advance) however, as many locals line the streets for launches.

Be aware that some of the attractions at the Kennedy Space Center Visitor Complex may be closed the day of a launch for safety reasons. Also, traffic can be unbearable after a launch, so plan to visit one of the many nearby beaches until roads are clear.

SHOPPING

There are gift shops at each of the stops on the bus tour, and a jumbo gift shop at the Visitor Center hub. Don't be shy—try the freeze-dried ice-cream sandwich or strawberries. You can also find snow globes, Space Shuttle gummy candy, T-shirts, and more. Prices vary from $2 for candy to $20 T-shirts.

DINING

Don't plan to grab breakfast (or any other meal) in the vicinity of Kennedy Space Center. It is very isolated, and there simply are not any restaurants within 20 miles. There are food locations on site, but they're nothing to cheer about. However, if you must eat, you'll find burgers and fries at The Lunch Pad and a wider selection in a food court at Orbit Restaurant. Mila's Roadhouse Grill offers more of a sit-down, full-service experience. There are also many food stands throughout the entire Kennedy Space Center Visitor Complex for a quick bite.

Part Five

SeaWorld

A world-class marine-life theme park, SeaWorld is the odd "middle child" of Central Florida's mega-parks—without the allure of Mickey Mouse or the glitz of the movie studio attractions.

For years, this park succeeded by appealing to those who appreciated the wonder of sea creatures like killer whales and dolphins. Disney World may have cornered the market on make-believe, but SeaWorld offered the unique opportunity of watching people interact with real, live animals.

As competition for tourists' time increased, and Disney ventured into the wild animal business with their Animal Kingdom, SeaWorld created new interactive encounters which can't be found at any other area park, and added thrill rides, including a flight simulator and roller coaster. Combined with the charm of the animals, these attractions and new, entertaining shows have created a whole new SeaWorld that isn't just for those intrigued by marine animals. It is even considered by many readers to be a favorite part of an Orlando vacation.

An English family writes:

The best organized park [is] SeaWorld. The computer printout we got on arrival had a very useful show schedule, told us which areas were temporarily closed due to construction and had a readily understandable map. Best of all, there was almost no queuing. Overall, we rated this day so highly that it is the park we would most like to visit again.

GETTING THERE

SeaWorld is located about 10 miles east of Walt Disney World. Take I-4 to FL 528 (Beeline Highway) east. Exit at the first ramp, which is International Drive. Turn left off exit ramp. Turn right at Central Florida Parkway. The entrance to SeaWorld is on the right just prior to a large SeaWorld sculpture. Parking is $6.

ADMISSION PRICES

Before purchasing tickets to SeaWorld, check out some of the choices below. The best option for most visitors is a one-day pass, which currently gets you in for a second day free (through the end of 1999). If you're planning to spend time at other local theme parks, consider the money-saving Orlando FlexTicket or the Adventure Passport. Discounts are available for AAA members, handicapped visitors, senior citizens, and military personnel.

One-day Pass
Adults: $44 + tax
Children (ages 3–9): $35
Children under age 3: Free
Two-day Pass
After December 31, 1999 a two-day pass is:
Adults: $54
Children: $45
Adventure Passport
(Five consecutive days at SeaWorld and Busch Gardens)
Adults: $79
Children: $64
Orlando FlexTicket
Three-park, Seven-day Pass
(Up to seven consecutive days at Universal Studios, SeaWorld, and Wet & Wild)
Adults: $159.95
Children: $127.95
Five-park, Ten-day Pass
(Up to ten consecutive days at Universal Studios, Islands of Adventure, SeaWorld, Wet & Wild, and Busch Gardens)
Adults: $196.95
Children (ages 3–9): $157.95

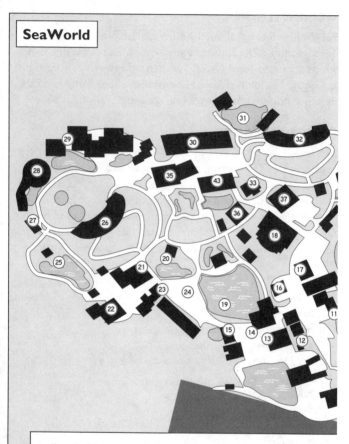

SeaWorld

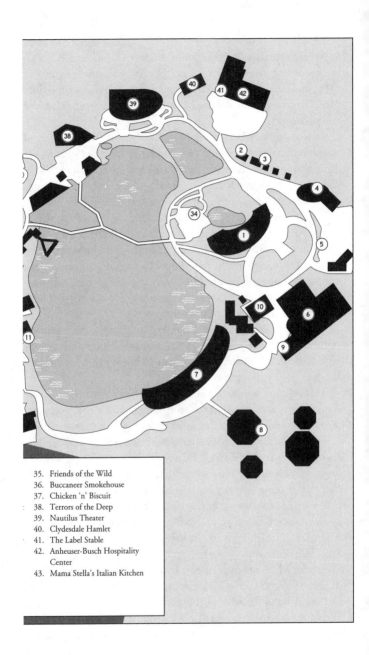

35. Friends of the Wild
36. Buccaneer Smokehouse
37. Chicken 'n' Biscuit
38. Terrors of the Deep
39. Nautilus Theater
40. Clydesdale Hamlet
41. The Label Stable
42. Anheuser-Busch Hospitality
    Center
43. Mama Stella's Italian Kitchen

ARRIVING

SeaWorld officially opens at 9 a.m. Ropes to a smaller section on the north side drop at 10 a.m., except during the busiest times of the year, when the entire park opens at once. Closing time fluctuates from 6 p.m. in fall and winter to 10 p.m. in the summer and on holidays.

Exploring SeaWorld takes a full day. Because the majority of attractions are shows, it won't be a mad rush to avoid lines like at other theme parks. However, seeing the few attractions with long waits and large crowds requires getting there early during busy times of the year. Like other area parks, SeaWorld turnstiles often open at either 8:30 or 8:45 a.m. depending on the season, which means you can enter the park before the scheduled 9 a.m. opening. You can only wander around a limited area, however, comprised of a bakery and a few shops. Nonetheless, during peak season, we suggest you arrive no later than 8:20 a.m., allowing time to park and purchase tickets. At other times, arriving at 8:40 a.m. should give you a jump on the crowds.

While a member of your party purchases tickets, have another track down a SeaWorld map. Map-toting employees are usually positioned in front of the ticket booth. While waiting for the park to open, plan your attack:

During peak season, if you're a fan of water thrill rides, locate the quickest route to Journey to Atlantis, which combines elements of a water ride and dry roller coaster. When the ropes drop, head straight there. You'll be tempted to stop at animal exhibits along the route, but don't. The line for Journey to Atlantis will be most manageable early in the day. In addition, many people find the thrilling Journey to Atlantis addictive, and riding twice is usually not feasible other than at park opening.

When attendance isn't at its highest, the lines for Journey to Atlantis can be quite short. At those times of the year, or if you don't like water rides, plan to hurry to Dolphin Cove in the Key West area when the park opens. In addition to beating the bulk of the crowd, the animals are most active in the morning. You can stand along the edge of this gorgeous two-acre pool teeming with dolphins to get a close-up view. But if the dolphins are one of your main reasons for visiting SeaWorld, use your morning visit to get the feeding schedule for the day, which is posted at the mint green fish house on the left side of the pool. There is usually a feeding scheduled at 9:15 a.m., and you can get in line to purchase fish right away.

Arrange the remainder of your day around the show schedule. Attractions circle a large lagoon and the best strategy to see it all is to travel clockwise, especially because the opposite side doesn't open until 10 a.m. (We've ordered the attractions listing in the clockwise order.) This tactic depends on the entertainment schedule, of course, but at the very least, allow time to see all the attractions in the area surrounding each show. You will save time and energy by not roaming the park and lower your stress level because the entertainment schedule is not designed for immediate back-to-back viewing of shows.

Walt Disney World might be known for its friendly, informative cast members, but they certainly haven't cornered the market. At each animal exhibit, you can find pleasant and extremely knowledgeable SeaWorld employees to share interesting information or to answer any questions.

SeaWorld also allows visitors to view training sessions that occur at many of the show stadiums. A schedule for these sessions isn't published, but if you're near any of the stadiums between shows, pop in. You can also hang out a bit after a show to possibly catch some unscripted action.

CONTACTING SEAWORLD

For more information, call (800) 327-2424, or visit the SeaWorld Web site at www.seaworld.com. If you or your children are interested in learning more about the park's animals before visiting, SeaWorld also maintains a web site designed for students and teachers at www.seaworld.org.

Attractions

Turtle Point

What It Is: Outdoor turtle habitat

Scope & Scale: Diversion

When to Go: Anytime, most informative when an educator is present

Author's Rating: ★★
Overall Appeal by Age Group:

Pre-school	Grade School	Teens	Young Adults	Over 30	Senior Citizens
★★	★★★	★★	★★	★★	★★

Description & Comments   A white sand beach and palm trees surround a small pool at this exhibit. Several large turtles can be seen swimming or sunning themselves. Most of them have been rescued by SeaWorld, and many of their injuries are evident, such as missing flippers (caused by discarded fishing line or shark attacks) or cracked shells (from boat propellers).

Touring Tips   Because the turtles are not terribly active, this attraction is only worth a quick peek. A visit becomes more exciting if an educator is present to talk about the animals and the ways humans can help protect them in the wild.

Stingray Lagoon   2.

What It Is: Stingray pool
Scope & Scale: Minor attraction
When to Go: Feeding times
Author's Rating: Interactive; ★★★
Overall Appeal by Age Group:

Pre-school	Grade School	Teens	Young Adults	Over 30	Senior Citizens
★★	★★★	★★★	★★★	★★★	★★★

Description & Comments   The shallow water in this waist-high pool is filled with dozens of undulating stingrays. They may seem menacing, but they are actually quite gentle, and you shouldn't be afraid to stick in your hands to feel their silky skin.

Touring Tips   Although a small tray of fish is $3, don't miss feeding these graceful creatures. (Feedings are scheduled throughout the day.) The fish are slimy, and the tail-end must be carefully placed between two fingers, but even the most squeamish in our group enjoyed the stingrays swimming over their hand and lightly sucking the food into their mouths.

Dolphin Cove

What It Is: Outdoor dolphin habitat

Scope & Scale: Major attraction

When to Go: In the morning; scheduled feedings throughout the day provide best opportunity to interact with the dolphins, but generate large crowds

Author's Rating: Impressive; ★★★★

Overall Appeal by Age Group:

Pre-school	Grade School	Teens	Young Adults	Over 30	Senior Citizens
★★½	★★★★	★★★★	★★★★	★★★★	★★★★

Description & Comments   This sprawling, two-acre habitat is filled with a community of swimming and leaping dolphins. You can stand along one side of the pool and touch or feed the dolphins, making this a unique experience you can't find at the hands-off Disney's Animal Kingdom. A path along the opposite side of the pool leads to an overlook area that provides excellent views and a great photo location. If you can live without touching the dolphins, this area is also much less crowded. Next to the overlook is a walkway to an underwater viewing area that provides the best glimpse of these delightful mammals in action.

Touring Tips   Feedings take place at scheduled times throughout the day, usually immediately following the dolphin show at nearby Key West Dolphin Stadium. Check the schedule at the fish house to the left of the pool. A small tray of fish is $3. Feedings provide the best opportunity to touch these amazing creatures, but the times may not fit into your plan to view the park. They are also incredibly crowded.

There is a chance you could touch the dolphins at other times. SeaWorld employees say the key is to simply keep your hands still under the water and patiently wait for the animals to brush into you. You may see SeaWorld trainers slapping the water to get the dolphins' attention, but this doesn't seem to work for guests. Apparently, the dolphins know and trust the trainers, but they are frightened by strange hands hitting the water.

*Show time
2 ✱*

Key West Dolphin Stadium/Key West Dolphin Fest

What It Is: Dolphin and pseudorca whale show

Scope & Scale: Major attraction

When to Go: Check daily entertainment schedule

Author's Rating: Excellent; ★★★★

Overall Appeal by Age Group:

Pre-school	Grade School	Teens	Young Adults	Over 30	Senior Citizens
★★★½	★★★★	★★★½	★★★★	★★★★	★★★★

Duration of Show: 25 minutes

Description & Comments   This lively show features Atlantic bottlenose dolphins and pseudorcas, or false killer whales. The dolphins perform incredible flips, twists, and jumps, some as high as 30 feet. There's also a segment that displays the relationship between the animals and trainers. One amusing portion involves a pint-sized volunteer who touches and interacts with a dolphin and is invited to jump in the water. Although the trainer is obviously joking, it's incredible how many kids actually begin to make the leap before being held back at the last possible moment.

Touring Tips   This stadium becomes packed quickly. Arrive early to get the best seats, although those at the top usually fill up last and provide a great overall view of the area. Best of all, the top of the stadium is shaded from the broiling sun. But if you do sit close, keep in mind the first three or four rows are in a "splash zone."

Key West Street Performers

What It Is: Variety performers

Scope & Scale: Diversion

When to Go: More frequent in the afternoon; all acts are out during a Sunset Celebration (check the daily schedule)

Author's Rating: Amusing; ★★½

Overall Appeal by Age Group:

Pre-school	Grade School	Teens	Young Adults	Over 30	Senior Citizens
★★★	★★★	★★½	★★½	★★½	★★★

Description & Comments   These street performers help create the Key West feel. They're a bit more sanitary than the variety you'd find in the actual party city, but every bit as entertaining. A gazebo in front of Stingray Lagoon features live bands performing beach music comprised mostly of Jimmy Buffett tunes. Other acts include fire eaters, jugglers, tight-rope walkers, and card tricksters. SeaWorld walk-around characters can usually be found in this area, as well.

Touring Tips   These performances provide a unique, relaxing break. If you're not in a hurry, grab a cool drink from the eatery just inside the entrance to Key West, find a seat, and chill out.

Manatees: The Last Generation?

What It Is: Outdoor manatee habitat and underwater viewing

Scope & Scale: Minor attraction

When to Go: Anytime

Author's Rating: Remarkable animals in a creative habitat; ★★★

Overall Appeal by Age Group:

Pre-school	Grade School	Teens	Young Adults	Over 30	Senior Citizens
★★½	★★★	★★★	★★★	★★★	★★★

Description & Comments   Manatees, which are on the endangered species list, are still disappearing at a rapid rate. All of the docile creatures in this exhibit were injured in the wild and have been rescued by SeaWorld. The area resembles an inland canal, a favorite spot of these gentle giants. For most of the rescued animals, this is the last part of their rehabilitation, and many will be returned to their natural environment.

Touring Tips   Be sure to visit the underwater viewing area. It offers an excellent view of these huge creatures. Along the way, you'll see a short video about the plight of these endangered animals.

On occasion, SeaWorld rescues orphaned baby manatees. Check with an educator in the area to find out if there are any in the exhibit, if they might be bottle fed, and at what time. It is a truly precious sight.

Journey to Atlantis

What It Is: Water ride and roller coaster combo

Scope & Scale: Headliner

When to Go: Before 10 a.m. or after 4 p.m. during peak season; avoid visiting immediately after a *Key West Dolphin Fest* show

Special Comments: Riders must be 42 inches tall; pregnant women
   or people with heart, back, or neck problems should not ride

Author's Rating: Quick, but thrilling; ★★★★

Overall Appeal by Age Group:

Pre-school	Grade School	Teens	Young Adults	Over 30	Senior Citizens
†	★★★★	★★★½	★★★★	★★★★	★★★

†*Preschoolers were generally too short to ride.*

Duration of Ride: 6 minutes

Loading Speed: Quick

Description & Comments Riders board eight-passenger boats and
plunge down a nearly vertical 60-foot waterfall before careening
through a mini–roller coaster. This combination of water ride and
dry roller coaster makes Journey to Atlantis a truly unique experience. The attraction supposedly takes guests on a voyage through
Atlantis as they try to avoid an evil spirit, but even after several
trips, we still didn't have a good grasp on this story line. For that
reason, and because of an "it's over before you know it" feeling,
we do give length and theming of the ride lower marks than those
of Disney's Splash Mountain. However, Journey to Atlantis definitely provides the biggest thrill.

Touring Tips Closer to sunset, the special effects in this attraction are much more intense because the darker evening sky
helps keep light from leaking into the ride when the boats travel
outdoors. However, during peak seasons the line can be as long
as an hour. Arrive early and be ready to dash to this attraction
when the park opens at 9 a.m. to avoid the wait. Then, stop by
in the evening and ride again if the line isn't too long. At less
crowded times, ride in the afternoon as the park doesn't usually
stay open past dark. During the cooler months, you'll appreciate
the warmth of the afternoon sun to help you dry off. During the
late spring and early fall, you'll be ready for a refreshing break
from the heat.

   As you've probably gathered from these last statements, you
will get wet, especially in the front seats. If that's not appealing,
don't let it stop you from riding. Simply bring along a poncho or
purchase one at the gift shop at the attraction. The ponchos will
keep you drier, but place any items that you don't want to get
soaked, such as cameras, in the pay lockers near the entrance to

the queue. (Free bins are available at the loading dock, but they are not locked.)

Don't miss the gorgeous Jewels of the Sea Aquarium to the right of the gift shop as you exit the ride. This is also an excellent place for those who don't brave Journey to Atlantis to wait for the rest of their party. Surprise someone by making them close their eyes as you lead them into the aquarium. When they take a peek, they'll be surrounded by fish—below, a glass floor reveals stingrays, and tropical fish and numerous sand sharks glide above. Press the button next to some of the aquariums in the walls to illuminate glowing jellyfish.

Kraken (opens spring 2000)

What It Is: Roller coaster

Scope & Scale: Headliner

When to Go: Immediately following a ride on Journey to Atlantis

Author's Rating: Not open at press time

Overall Appeal by Age Group: Not open at press time

Duration of Ride: A little more than 3½ minutes

Loading Speed: Quick

Description & Comments A coaster war has reached epidemic proportions in central Florida. SeaWorld will enter the battle in Spring 2000 with Kraken, named after a mythological underwater beast. At a top speed of 65 miles per hour, a length of more than 4,000 feet, and with a first drop of 144 feet, it will be Orlando's fastest, longest, and tallest roller coaster when it premiers. However, with the ongoing thrill-ride saga in O-town, we don't expect it to remain that way for long.

This coaster is hard to describe. Designers call it "floorless," with 32 open-sided seats in eight rows riding on a pedestal, high above the track. Riders' feet dangle and there is nothing above their heads. There will be seven loops, and plans call for the coaster to dive underground three times.

Touring Tips This attraction will be extremely popular. Ride before 10 a.m. or after 4 p.m. During peak season, we suggest you arrive when the park opens, ride Journey to Atlantis, and immediately head to Kraken. After getting drenched, the high-speed coaster trip will help dry you off.

Penguin Encounter

What It Is: Indoor penguin habitat

Scope & Scale: Major attraction

When to Go: Anytime

Author's Rating: Adorable; ★★★

Overall Appeal by Age Group:

Pre-school	Grade School	Teens	Young Adults	Over 30	Senior Citizens
★★★½	★★★	★★★	★★★	★★★	★★★

Description & Comments   The first section of this exhibit features an icy habitat behind a glass wall that provides an excellent view of the penguins' antics in several feet of water. Step on the people mover to the right for a close-up view of these "tuxedo-clad" creatures as they congregate, waddle, and dive into the frigid water. Then circle back behind the people mover to an elevated section where you can take a longer look at the large king penguins. A learning area is just past the habitat, where interactive kiosks provide information about the animals and their environment. The walkway then leads to a smaller exhibit, which is home to species that prefer a warmer climate, including puffins.

Touring Tips   Their pungent odor will hit you before you step through the door, but the sight of these cute creatures makes it worthwhile, and after a few minutes your nose becomes accustomed to the smell.

During summer, SeaWorld darkens the exhibit to simulate the Antarctic environment, where it is actually winter. The birds are still active and visible, but you may need to spend more time on the stationary upper level to get a good look. You also will not be allowed to shoot any photos of the habitat because the flash negates the effect of the darkened room for the animals.

Pacific Point Preserve

What It Is: Outdoor sea lion habitat

Scope & Scale: Major attraction

When to Go: Feeding time (scattered throughout day)

Author's Rating: Amusing; ★★★

Overall Appeal by Age Group:

Pre-school	Grade School	Teens	Young Adults	Over 30	Senior Citizens
★★★½	★★★½	★★★	★★★	★★★	★★★

Description & Comments Let the sound of more than 50 barking sea lions and harbor seals lead you to this nifty area tucked behind Sea Lion & Otter Stadium. An elevated walkway behind a glass partition surrounds the sunken habitat. The animals can be found sunning themselves on the rocky terrain or lounging in the shallow waves. More often though, they'll be barking impatiently for a snack. Although these animals aren't trained, a few of the sea lions will improvise cute antics for food, such as mimicking you sticking out your tongue.

Touring Tips If you participate in a feeding, which costs $3 for one tray of fish (or $5 for two), watch out for the large birds that lurk in this area. They are poised to steal the fish right out of your hand or snatch one in mid-air as you toss it to the sea lions.

Look closely at the animals, and you might spot some adorable sea lion or harbor seal pups—especially if you visit during the spring or summer.

Sea Lion & Otter Stadium/*Clyde & Seamore Take Pirate Island*

Show ✱

What It Is: Show featuring sea lions, otters, and a walrus

Scope & Scale: Major attraction

When to Go: Check daily entertainment schedule

Author's Rating: Quite funny; ★★★½

Overall Appeal by Age Group:

Pre-school	Grade School	Teens	Young Adults	Over 30	Senior Citizens
★★★	★★★½	★★★	★★★½	★★★½	★★★½

Description & Comments SeaWorld's famous sea lion duo, Clyde and Seamore, are the stars of this corny, but funny show. The plot has the pair looking for a treasure map that's been swiped by an adorable tiny otter. During the search, the sea lions' antics are quite entertaining, as they mimic their trainers and leap, flip, and swan dive into the narrow pool in front of the stage. The trainers get in on the act with slapstick humor, especially when the animals don't quite cooperate. For the finale, an enormous walrus makes an appearance. Look out if you're in the front center rows because this guy sometimes spits a few mouthfuls of water, and his aim and projection are excellent.

Touring Tips   Arrive early, not only to get a good seat but to enjoy a preshow that's almost as much fun as the actual performance. A ruthless, but incredibly funny mime pokes fun at unsuspecting visitors entering the stadium. During one visit, the mime created a elaborately panicked chase scene with a guest in a fast-moving electric wheelchair, who happily joined in the act. The chase ended in mock showdown of mime and man.

SeaWorld Theater/Pets on Stage

What It Is: Show featuring trained pets

Scope & Scale: Major attractions

When to Go: Check daily entertainment schedule

Author's Rating: Amusing; ★★★

Overall Appeal by Age Group:

Pre-school	Grade School	Teens	Young Adults	Over 30	Senior Citizens
★★½	★★★	★★½	★★★	★★★	★★★

Description & Comments   Most people don't immediately think of trained dogs and cats when they think of SeaWorld, but this show holds the charm of the rest of the park sans the water. *Pets on Stage* stars a menagerie of trained animals from frisky felines to a precious pig. You'll be amazed at what these animals can do. You'll be doubly amazed at the fact that most were rescued from an uncertain fate at local animal shelters.

Touring Tips   Be sure to arrive early. Because many of the animals perform throughout the theater, doors close promptly at show time. Be sure to stick around afterward to meet a few of the star performers at the foot of the stage.

Sky Tower

What It Is: Scenic aerial ride

Scope & Scale: Minor attraction

When to Go: Anytime, although it's quite beautiful at night

Special Comments: Costs $3

Author's Rating: A treat if you don't mind the extra charge; ★★½

Overall Appeal by Age Group:

Pre-school	Grade School	Teens	Young Adults	Over 30	Senior Citizens
★★	★★	★★	★★½	★★½	★★★

Duration of Ride: Nearly seven minutes

Loading Speed: Slow

Description & Comments   This attraction forces visitors to make a philosophical decision. Should a theme park charge an additional fee for one of its rides? Although the answer is probably "no," a ride to the top is somewhat calming. The tower has two levels of enclosed seats that rotate as they rise to the top for great views of the park. It's amazing how serene the park looks—and how tiny the killer whales appear—from the top. On a clear day, you can see many other interesting sites, including downtown Orlando, the top of Spaceship Earth at Epcot, and the unmistakable toaster shape of Disney's Contemporary Resort.

Touring Tips   This attraction closes if lightning or high winds pop up, and both are frequent in central Florida. It also doesn't run during the nighttime fireworks displayed in peak seasons.

Terrors of the Deep

What It Is: Animal exhibit

Scope & Scale: Major attraction

When to Go: Anytime

Author's Rating: Terror-ific; ★★★★

Overall Appeal by Age Group:

Pre-school	Grade School	Teens	Young Adults	Over 30	Senior Citizens
★★★	★★★★	★★★★	★★★★	★★★★	★★★★

Description & Comments   This exhibit immerses you in the frightening world of dangerous marine life. First, you are surrounded by moray eels as you walk through an acrylic tube at the bottom of a large aquarium. These creepy creatures stick their heads out of large holes in an artificial tropical reef or slither through the water. Next are several large aquariums featuring poisonous fish, including the beautiful but lethal scorpion fish and the puffer fish, one of the world's most deadly. Then get ready for the grand finale—a 600,000-gallon tank filled with six different species of sharks, including bull sharks, nurse sharks, and lemon sharks, as well as dozens of enormous grouper and other smaller fish. An entire wall of a large rooms gives an overall view of this beautifully lit tank. Then these amazing creatures will glide next to you and directly over head as you pass through a 124-foot acrylic tunnel. As you exit the tunnel, you'll learn that it supports 450 tons of salt water, but if necessary, it could handle nearly five times that weight, the equivalent of more than 370 elephants.

Touring Tips   The crowd usually bottlenecks at the eel habitat. If possible, slither—like an eel—through the initial backup. The tube is fairly long, and you'll find the same great view with a smaller crowd near the end.

If you visit SeaWorld on a Tuesday or Thursday, don't miss the feeding frenzy when the sharks in the main habitat feast at 11 a.m. (call beforehand to verify the schedule).

You can get in on the feeding yourself on select days at a small pool at the entrance to the exhibit. Purchase a tray of fish for $3 (two for $5) and toss them to small hammerhead and nurse sharks.

Nautilus Theater/*Cirque de la Mer*

What It Is: New-age, circus-type acts

Scope & Scale: Major attraction

When to Go: Check daily entertainment schedule

Author's Rating: Interesting and entertaining; ★★★

Overall Appeal by Age Group:

Pre-school	Grade School	Teens	Young Adults	Over 30	Senior Citizens
★★	★★½	★★	★★★	★★★	★★★

Duration of Show: 30 minutes

Description & Comments   Much like the sea lion show, this performance features a preshow mime that ridicules and jeers audience members. But as the show starts, the mime is drawn through the curtains and becomes the show's silent host. The performance features an amazing group of variety acts, including a brawny male acrobatic duo that performs a series of mind-boggling lifts and gymnastic poses balanced on a small platform. Another scene showcases a couple who fly and twist through the air suspended by two long sheets of cloth. This succession of performers deserves top billing, but a major highlight are the mime's comic interludes, including a hilarious mock boxing match with five unsuspecting audience volunteers. While it's hard to compare a theme park show with the full-scale production of Cirque du Soleil at Downtown Disney, this show does capture the circus-as-theater element for those who cannot afford the steep price tag at Disney World.

Touring Tips   This indoor, air-conditioned theater rarely fills up, but we suggest you arrive early to enjoy the preshow and a pleasant break from the Florida heat. Also, once your group gets settled, use the time for a rest room break. They're conveniently located at the back of the theater. In addition, this show is not performed two days of the week. If it's a priority, call to verify.

Clydesdale Hamlet/Hospitality Center

What It Is: Stable and free beer

Scope & Scale: Diversion

When to Go: Avoid visiting immediately following Cirque de la Mer or a Shamu show

Author's Rating: Most kids will enjoy the horses, most adults will enjoy the beer; ★★½

Overall Appeal by Age Group:

Pre-school	Grade School	Teens	Young Adults	Over 30	Senior Citizens
★★½	★★★	★★	★★½	★★½	★★★

Description & Comments   An Anheuser-Busch theme park, Sea-World features a white stable that is home to several Clydesdales, a huge and beautiful draft horse that is the beer company's mascot. Walk through the stable on the way to the Hospitality House. Here, if you're age 21 or older, you can partake in two free samples of Anheuser-Busch beer. You can also sign up for Budweiser Beer School, a free 40-minute class on beer making, which includes a variety of samples.

Touring Tips   The Clydesdales are incredibly beautiful animals, but skip this area if you're in a hurry. Also, check the entertainment schedule for appearances of the Clydesdales in the park.

The Hospitality House also features The Deli. Save time by combining lunch with your free beer sample.

Shamu Stadium/*The Shamu Adventure*

What It Is: Killer whale show

Scope & Scale: Super headliner

When to Go: Check daily entertainment schedule, first show is
sometimes more crowded

Author's Rating: Truly amazing, not to be missed; ★★★★½

Overall Appeal by Age Group:

Pre-school	Grade School	Teens	Young Adults	Over 30	Senior Citizens
★★★★	★★★★½	★★★★	★★★★½	★★★★½	★★★★½

Duration of Show: 25 minutes

Description & Comments   Fog rolls over the pool and ominous
music fills the stadium as this show begins. Beyond a six-foot-
high clear wall, an immense killer whale circles in a five-million-
gallon pool. Jack Hanna, on a large video screen elevated the water,
introduces the whales and keeps the show flowing with information about their environment and feeding habits. The real stars
of this show are a family of orcas, commonly known as killer
whales. Like any celebrity, they're known by stage names—most
notably, Shamu and Baby Shamu.

Of course, the trainers and whales work closely and jointly
provide the most spectacular sight of the show—a trainer perched
on the nose of a whale shooting nearly 30 feet out of the water.
The trusting relationship they build is also evident when a trainer
surfs on a whale's back, is pushed through the water on a whale's
nose, or circles, hand on flipper in the water.

If these huge creatures' leaps and arcs are the most spectacular portion of the show, a display of their incredibly power is the
most stunning—or should we say numbing! This is when gallons
of 55-degree salt water are flung into the first 14 rows by the rear
fluke of a large whale. The audience is warned, but most folks
must not realize how much water will head their way or how cold
it really is. Nevertheless, some, especially the under age 12 set,
make it a point to be in the water's path.

Now, this sight is incredible, but the most astonishing scene
is yet to come . . . when a five-ton whale, the largest in captivity,
makes his splashing rounds. Not only do the folks in the first 14
rows get soaked, but the water actually travels an extra 15–20 feet
to reach the second tier of this large stadium.

Touring Tips   We're not kidding when we say gallons of chilly salt water. You will get soaked in the first few rows. If you or the kids think you're up for it, you might want to bring along some extra clothes to change into after the cold shower. You should also leave your cameras and electronic equipment with someone out of the range of the corrosive salt water.

Although this is a large stadium, you must arrive early to get a seat. Jack Hanna will keep you entertained with a video pop quiz. Audience members are amusingly caught off guard by their image on the screen and must answer a multiple-choice question.

Shamu Stadium/*Shamu Rocks America*   ✳ Night

What It Is: Nighttime killer whale show

Scope & Scale: Headliner

When to Go: Check daily entertainment schedule

Author's Rating: Excellent; ★★★★

Overall Appeal by Age Group:

Pre-school	Grade School	Teens	Young Adults	Over 30	Senior Citizens
★★★★	★★★★	★★★★	★★★★	★★★★	★★★★

Duration of Show: 25 minutes

Description & Comments   Think Shamu at a 1970s rock concert without the long hair and drugs. Nonetheless, this show is extremely entertaining. The whales take center stage—no excessive narration or audience participation, just a few of the most exciting stunts from *The Shamu Adventure* set to great music. This show also has a more carefree feel than the daytime shows. A fun blooper clip is shown on the video screen, and Shamu does some cute "dance" moves as he bobs and shakes to the music.

Touring Tips   This is a fun counterpart to *The Shamu Adventure* and a nice conclusion to your day. However, if you're pinched for time and can't see both shows, choose the daytime performance. It's filled with more interesting information about the animals. An exception might be during peak times when the park is open later and *Shamu Rocks America* is performed after sunset. Then the show is magic with a spotlight on Shamu, colored lights scanning the audience, and the pool glowing aqua and green.

Just as with *The Shamu Adventure,* you will get soaked with chilly salt water in the first 14 rows of the stadium.

Shamu Close Up!

What It Is: Whale viewing area

Scope & Scale: Minor attraction

When to Go: Avoid visiting immediately before or after a Shamu show

Author's Rating: Excellent look at these incredible animals; ★★★

Overall Appeal by Age Group:

Pre-school	Grade School	Teens	Young Adults	Over 30	Senior Citizens
★★	★★★	★★★	★★★	★★★	★★★

Description & Comments   Go "behind the scenes" at Shamu stadium for a peek at the stars of the show in this 1.5-million-gallon pool. Check the above-water viewing area for a training session or a veterinary visit. When standing "next to" these animals in the underwater viewing area, be prepared to be awestruck by their enormous size.

Touring Tips   When the animals are not active, or not even present, this area is not worth visiting. Check with the SeaWorld employee usually stationed in this area for the best times to visit on a particular day.

Have your camera ready in the underwater viewing area. The whales usually slowly circle the pool, offering an amazing backdrop for a group photo.

Shamu's Happy Harbor

What It Is: Children's play area

Scope & Scale: Minor attraction

When to Go: Avoid visiting after a Shamu show

Special Comments: Open from 10 a.m. until an hour before the park closes

Author's Rating: A nice oversized playground; ★★★

Overall Appeal by Age Group:

Pre-school	Grade School	Teens	Young Adults	Over 30	Senior Citizens
★★★	★★★	★★	★★	★★	★

Description & Comments   Four stories of net span this three-acre children's play area. Children and brave adults can climb, crawl, and weave through this net "jungle." Other activities include an air bubble where kids under 54 inches tall can bounce and play and an interactive submarine with several water cannons and fountains. There is also an area for smaller kids (they must be under 42 inches tall) with a room filled with small plastic balls and several playground contraptions.

Touring Tips   Parents can grab a cool drink and relax at Coconut Cove while watching their children play. Most adults should stay clear of the patience-testing, headache-causing steel drum area, where kids are allowed to bang to their hearts' content.

Wild Arctic

What It Is: Simulator ride and animal exhibit

Scope & Scale: Major attraction

When to Go: Avoid going immediately following a Shamu show; wait will be shorter before 11 a.m. and after 4 p.m.

Author's Rating: Intriguing animals, wonderful presentation; ★★★★

Overall Appeal by Age Group:

Pre-school	Grade School	Teens	Young Adults	Over 30	Senior Citizens
★★★	★★★★	★★★★	★★★★	★★★★	★★★★

Duration of Ride: 5 minutes for simulator; at your own pace for exhibit

Loading Speed: Moderate

Description & Comments   Wild Arctic combines an excellent simulator ride and a spectacular animal habitat, featuring huge polar bears, blubbery walruses, and sweet beluga whales. The usually long line gives you the option of not riding the simulator and heading straight to the animal habitat—a great idea if you're in a hurry or get motion sick.

The simulator provides a bumpy ride aboard a specially designed 59-passenger "helicopter." Once safely strapped in, the ride takes visitors to a remote research station. On the way, riders "fly over" polar bear and walrus, and even find themselves in the middle of a life-threatening avalanche.

As you step off the simulator, or if you bypass it, you'll enter a cavernous, fog-filled room. A walkway on the far side overlooks a large pool that is home to a few beluga whales and, if you're lucky, some adorable harbor seals. This room sets the Arctic mood, but unless it's feeding time the animals rarely surface.

Proceed down a wooden ramp and you may come face to face with an enormous polar bear. The most famous inhabitants of this exhibit are twins, Klondike and Snow. The duo received tons of media coverage after they were abandoned by their mother and hand-raised at the Denver Zoo. SeaWorld uses toys and enrichment devices to keep the bears occupied. Variations in their schedule help keep them on their toes, so feeding times change frequently. Next to the bears are the gigantic walruses. These animals are often lounging near the glass or lazily swimming.

As you descend further into the exhibit, you'll discover an incredible underwater viewing area. Swarms of fish circle in the polar bear exhibit. If you're lucky, you'll catch a bear diving for fish. See if you can spot Snow, the female twin, carefully planning her attack as she hovers, waiting for the right moment to go in for the kill. If it's Klondike or one of the other males, you'll more than likely find him clumsily swiping at the fish. In addition, the underwater view will give you the big picture of the walruses' size. If it's quiet you can also hear the deep vocalizations of these large beasts. This is also the best location to catch a glimpse of the beluga whales. Looking like puffy, bulbous dolphins, these gentle creatures glide through the water. On occasion, a few playful harbor seals will join them. These crazy critters will come right up to the glass for a staring match with you.

Touring Tips As in all animal exhibits, several SeaWorld educators are scattered around to answer any questions. (If you're interested, they can also point out whether Klondike or Snow are in the habitat.) Here, they are easy to spot in bright red parkas.

The simulator holds nearly 60 riders, who flood the animal area after each trip. Hang back behind the crowd for a few minutes, waiting for them to clear. Then you can have the area mostly to yourself until the next group dumps off the ride.

Entering through the gift shop to the right of the attraction entrance is a quick way to bypass the ride but still see the animals. There is a sign that says "no reentry," but we were never stopped. Just work your way to the back of the shop and walk down a winding ramp to the exhibit. You'll start in the underwater area, so don't forget to head up top to see the polar bears above water.

Atlantis Bayside Stadium/*Intensity Water Ski Show*

What It Is: Water-ski show

Scope & Scale: Headliner

When to Go: Check daily entertainment schedule

Author's Rating: Exciting; ★★★★

Overall Appeal by Age Group:

Pre-school	Grade School	Teens	Young Adults	Over 30	Senior Citizens
★★★½	★★★★	★★★★	★★★★	★★★★	★★★

Duration of Show: 30 minutes

Description & Comments   Athletes on jet skis, wakeboards, and water skis perform incredible stunts at dizzying speeds. On land, gymnasts tumble, flip, and play basketball on trampolines. The athletes compete against each other on Pepsi and Mountain Dew teams. While this is a blatant plug for the official soft drink of SeaWorld, the competition element helps tie the show together better than its counterpart at Cypress Gardens. However, the Cypress Gardens show does contain a greater variety of acts, and has a long-standing water-ski history in its favor.

Touring Tips   This stadium is huge, and all seats, even in the second tier, provide great views. Unlike other SeaWorld shows, the preshow consists only of the athletes warming up, so there's no need to arrive early.

If you do take the stairs to the balcony, be aware that you cannot walk freely from one section to the next in this level. We suggest you go up the stairs near the middle of the stadium to find a center-stage seat.

Luau Terrace/*Hawaiian Rhythms*

What It Is: Luau show

Scope & Scale: Minor attraction

When to Go: Check daily entertainment schedule

Author's Rating: Amusing; ★★½

Overall Appeal by Age Group:

Pre-school	Grade School	Teens	Young Adults	Over 30	Senior Citizens
★★	★★	★½	★★½	★★½	★★★

Duration of Show: 25 minutes

Description & Comments   This show features a fire juggler, grass-skirted dancers, and musicians performing traditional Polynesian numbers. The 1970s-era theater needs an update, but the show provides low-key humor and entertainment. In a particularly amusing segment, several male audience members are chosen to play the drums and hula with the dancers. A bar serves snacks and beverages, including frozen drinks that can create an annoying buzz in the sound system when the blender is in high gear.

Touring Tips   This is a tiny theater, so arrive early.

Luau Terrace/*Aloha Polynesian Luau*

What It Is: Nightly dinner show
Scope & Scale: Major attraction
When to Go: Seating begins at 6:30 p.m.
Special Comments: Added cost; see below
Author's Rating: Nice; ★★★½
Overall Appeal by Age Group:

Pre-school	Grade School	Teens	Young Adults	Over 30	Senior Citizens
★★½	★★★	★★½	★★★½	★★★½	★★★★

Duration of Show: Two hours

Description & Comments   This nightly dinner features an extended version of the daytime performance and a menu of mahi mahi, smoked pork, sweet and sour chicken, vegetables, salad, and fresh fruit. The food isn't exceptional, but comparable to most local dinner shows.

Price, including a free cocktail, is $35.95 for adults (age 13 and above), $25.95 for juniors (ages 8–12), and $15.95 for kids.

Touring Tips   Advanced reservations are required and can be made by calling (800) 327-2424. If you are in the park, check in at the Luau reservation counter near the front entrance. You can see the Luau without visiting the park if you'd like to save it for another day.

Dolphin Nursery

What It Is: Outdoor pool for expecting dolphins or moms and calves
Scope & Scale: Diversion

When to Go: Anytime

Author's Rating: Only a quick glimpse is necessary unless a baby is present; ★★

Overall Appeal by Age Group:

Pre-school	Grade School	Teens	Young Adults	Over 30	Senior Citizens
★	★★	★	★★	★★	★★

Description & Comments   Seeing this tiny pool that used to be the sole dolphin experience at SeaWorld should make you appreciate Dolphin Cove all the more. But the small size is perfect for its current purpose—providing a seperate area for pregnant dolphins and new moms and calves. Stop by for a quick glance if it's an expecting dolphin. Stay longer if there is a baby in the pool.

Touring Tips   This area will be roped off and guests understandably kept away when a dolphin goes into labor. Because it's near the park entrance, swing by on your way out to see if the area has reopened and you might be able to view mom and baby.

Hiding next to the Dolphin Nursery is one of the most beautiful and secluded areas of SeaWorld. Find the path next to the nursery and enter a lush tropical rain forest. A large banyan tree and 30-foot-tall bamboo trees shade the entire area. Large fish swim in a small pond, and two beautiful macaws perch on a branch. There is also an aviary featuring blue dacnis and red-legged honeycreepers, both adorably tiny birds. There are no formal benches, but a few stone ledges provide the perfect place to get away from the sun and the theme-park hustle and bustle.

Tropical Reef

What It Is: Indoor aquariums/outdoor tide pool

Scope & Scale: Diversion

When to Go: Anytime; skip if you're in a hurry

Author's Rating: ★★

Overall Appeal by Age Group:

Pre-school	Grade School	Teens	Young Adults	Over 30	Senior Citizens
★	★★½	★	★★	★★	★★½

Description & Comments   A small outdoor tide pool is home to several sea urchins, sea cucumber, and spiny lobster. It's not much to look at, but visitors are encouraged to stick their hands in and touch the urchins, which is a fun experience. Inside, hundreds of tropical fish swim in numerous aquariums. The aquariums are set into the walls, so the colorful fish are only visible through the front pane of glass. Information and interesting facts can be found on lighted signs near each aquarium.

Touring Tips   Fish lovers should definitely visit. Others might want to spend more time in some of the more interactive animal exhibits. It is extremely dark in the indoor display. Stand aside and let your eyes adjust to avoid bumping into other visitors.

Nighttime Show

What It Is: Laser and fireworks show
Scope & Scale: Major attraction
When to Go: Check daily entertainment schedule
Special Comments: Only displayed during peak seasons
Author's Rating: ★★★
Overall Appeal by Age Group:

Pre-school	Grade School	Teens	Young Adults	Over 30	Senior Citizens
★★★	★★★	★★★	★★★	★★★	★★★

Description & Comments   During summer and on holidays, this laser and fireworks show explodes over the lagoon in front of Bayside Stadium. The theme of the show changes frequently, most recently featuring a patriotic salute. No matter the theme, the show features common elements, including fireworks, lasers, and film projection on a water curtain in the lagoon—all set to music. While the show might not be quite as spectacular as IllumiNations, it is a great fireworks display and the projections on the water screen are unique.

Touring Tips   A pleasant difference from Disney's nighttime shows, there's no need to stake a spot hours in advance. We recommend arriving about 15 minutes early. In addition, you won't be stuck standing up or with tree-blocked views, because the action is easily seen from the comfortable stadium seats.

Sitting on the bottom level provides the best view of the fireworks, but the second tier offers a great overall view of the water screens and lasers. If you do sit in the second level, be aware that you cannot easily move between sections on this level. We suggest you go up the stairs near the middle of the stadium to find a center-stage seat.

GUIDED TOURS

What It Is: Behind-the-scenes tours

Scope & Scale: Headliner

When to Go: Check education counter for schedule

Special Comments: Cost $6.95 for adults, $5.95 for children ages 3–9

Author's Rating: ★★★½

Overall Appeal by Age Group:

Pre-school	Grade School	Teens	Young Adults	Over 30	Senior Citizens
★★½	★★★½	★★½	★★★½	★★★½	★★★★

Description & Comments These 60-minute tours are extremely informative and entertaining, and worth the additional charge.

To the Rescue!

Go behind-the-scenes for a fascinating look at SeaWorld's animal rescue and rehabilitation efforts. There are usually several injured manatees and sea turtles in a backstage area comprised of three manatee pools and several isolated turtle pools. SeaWorld has also rescued seals and aquatic birds.

Sharks!

Get a back-stage view of the sharks at Terrors of the Deep while learning how SeaWorld staff cares for these dangerous creatures. The tour includes a visit to the shark food preparation room and the chance to touch a live shark.

Polar Expedition Tour

Encounter a magellanic penguin face to face and visit SeaWorld's Penguin Research Facility. Then get a peek at the Wild Arctic support areas, where SeaWorld prepares food and enrichment devices for the polar bears.

Touring Tips   Advance reservations are not accepted for these tours. You must stop by the guided tour counter at the front of the park on the day of your visit. Arriving early is important because you sign up on a first come, first served basis.

Taking an hour out of your visit to SeaWorld for these tours will require careful planning or possibly returning for a second day to see the rest of the park.

EXTENDED BEHIND-THE-SCENES PROGRAMS

Dolphin Interaction Program

(Will be discontinued sometime prior to the Discovery Cove opening in spring 2000)

What It Is: Half-day session with dolphin interaction

Scope & Scale: Headliner

When to Go: Education department provides schedule

Special Comments: Costs $159; participants must be at least 10 years old

Author's Rating: Expensive, but a great experience; ★★★★

Overall Appeal by Age Group:

Pre-school	Grade School	Teens	Young Adults	Over 30	Senior Citizens
†	★★★★	★★★★	★★★★	★★★★	★★★

†Preschoolers are not old enough.

Description & Comments   The session begins with a class on Sea-World techniques for caring for and training dolphins. Then squeeze into a wetsuit and wade into the main pool with the trainers at Key West Dolphin Stadium for a face-to-face encounter with dolphins.

Touring Tips   Admission is limited, so it's best to call up to six months ahead. However, there is the possibility of last-minute openings due to cancellations. Call (407) 370-1385 for information and reservations.

Trainer for a Day

What It Is: Chance to shadow a SeaWorld trainer for a day

Scope & Scale: Headliner

When to Go: Program begins at 7 a.m.

Special Comments: Costs $349; participants must be at least 13 years old

Author's Rating: Extremely expensive, but worth it if you can afford it; ★★★★

Overall Appeal by Age Group:

Pre-school	Grade School	Teens	Young Adults	Over 30	Senior Citizens
†	†	★★★★	★★★★	★★★★	★★★

†Preschoolers and grade school kids are not old enough.

Description & Comments Shadow a SeaWorld trainer during this eight-hour program. Learn through hands-on experience how SeaWorld staff members care for and train their animals, from stuffing vitamins into a slimy fish to positive-reinforcement training techniques. The fee includes a "Trainer for a Day" T-shirt, waterproof disposable camera, and lunch with the trainers.

Touring Tips Attendance for this program is limited to three people per day. Again, calling up to six months ahead is best, but cancellations do occur. For information and reservations, call (407) 370-1382. Participants must be in good physical condition and at least 13 years old.

SHOPPING

Unlike at Disney, shopping at SeaWorld isn't an attraction in and of itself. There is, of course, a huge selection of SeaWorld merchandise. Some of it is unique, and prices are relatively reasonable. Fans of ocean wildlife can find a vast array of marine merchandise, ranging from high-quality, expensive sculptures to T-shirts, beach towels, and knickknacks. Children will be overwhelmed by the huge selection of stuffed animals, and parents will be pleased by their low prices—many small- to medium-sized toys for under $10. Budweiser enthusiasts will enjoy the large selection of Anheuser-Busch merchandise, including beer mugs, caps, and nice golf shirts.

DINING

SeaWorld offers much more than the usual theme park fare of burger and fries. The food for the most part is very good and prices are a bit lower than Disney World's.

Your feasting can begin at Cypress Bakery, which opens at 8:30 a.m. during the busy season and at 8:45 a.m. otherwise. Choose from a dizzying array of wonderful pastries, cakes, and muffins to enjoy while you plan your day.

For a sit-down meal, there's Bimini Bay Café, which features salads, sandwiches, pasta, chicken, or fish. Portions are large and an average meal will cost about $10–15.

For quick service, try Mango Joe's Cafe for fajitas, salads, and sandwiches; Mama Stella's Italian Kitchen for pasta and pizza; or barbecue at Buccaneer Smokehouse. Another favorite: the hand-carved sandwiches at The Deli in the Hospitality House.

Discovery Cove (opening summer 2000)

Fueled by a large number of requests to swim with the dolphins and the popularity of the Dolphin Interaction Program, SeaWorld is creating Discovery Cove, an interactive marine-life park, scheduled to open in summer 2000. Visitors will be able to swim with dolphins, stingrays, and tropical fish. They will also encounter hundreds of tropical birds, as well as sharks and barracuda, which will swim in a separate area behind glass.

Described as a series of rocky lagoons surrounded by landscaping, waterfalls, and beaches, the 30-acre park is located on Central Florida Parkway, directly across from the SeaWorld entrance. SeaWorld claims there will be no lines or need to rush for any activities because admission is by reservation only and will be limited. The exact number of guests and price tag were not available at press time, but SeaWorld estimates 1,000 guests per day will pay $150–$250 each. The price tag is steep, but the experience will be quite unique. The cost will also include lunch and guest amenities, including snorkeling gear, towels, lockers, and beach umbrellas (drinks and snacks are extra). A personal guide will also provide an orientation and tour.

You must make reservations to visit Discovery Cove. For more information and reservations, call (877) 434-7268. SeaWorld also has developed an extremely informative, interactive Web site for Discovery Cove at www.discoverycove.com.

What You Can Expect to Find at Discovery Cove

Dolphin Lagoon   Be among three guests and a trainer to wade into a lagoon and be introduced to a dolphin. Then swim and play with the animal one-on-one. The experience also includes an opportunity to learn about dolphin behavior and communicating with the animals using hand signals.

Coral Reef   Don snorkeling gear and swim with 10,000 tropical fish in an artificial coral reef. Species include angelfish, butterfly fish, silvery jacks, and spadefish.

Stingray Lagoon   Snorkel, wade, and play with hundreds of southern and cownose stingrays. As with the Stingray Lagoon in Key West at SeaWorld, these animals may look menacing, but are extremely gentle. Some can grow up to four feet in diameter.

Tropical River   This waterway winds through most of the park. Snorkel through different areas, including an island beach, tropical forest, Amazon-like river, fishing village, and underwater cave.

Aviary   Swim through a waterfall along the tropical river and find yourself in a 100-foot-long, 35-foot-tall aviary. The naturalistic exhibit, resembling a tropical forest, houses 300 tropical birds. The 30 species on display include tawny frogmouths, roseate spoonbills, turacos, thrushes, and starlings.

Part Six

Universal Florida

Disney-MGM Studios vs. Universal Studios Florida

Disney-MGM Studios and Universal Studios Florida are direct competitors. Because both are large and expensive and require at least one day to see, some guests must choose one park over the other. While Disney-MGM opened almost two years before Universal Studios Florida, Universal is currently involved in a major expansion project that may give the park a leg up over Disney-MGM. In the summer of 1999, Universal launched its second major theme park, Universal's Islands of Adventure, which has no direct Disney competitor. The new park is previewed in detail later in this section.

Both Disney-MGM Studios and Universal Studios Florida draw their theme and inspiration from film and television. Both offer movie- and TV-themed rides and shows, some of which are just for fun, while others provide an educational, behind-the-scenes introduction to the cinematic arts. Both parks include working film and television production studios.

Nearly half of Disney-MGM Studios is off-limits to guests except by guided tour, while virtually all of Universal Studios Florida is open to exploration. Unlike Disney-MGM, Universal Florida's open area includes the entire backlot, where guests can walk at leisure among movie sets.

Universal hammers on the point that it's first a working motion-picture and television studio, and only incidentally a tourist attraction. Whether this assertion is a point of pride with Universal or an apology to the tourist is unclear. It's true, however, that guests are more likely to see movie or television production in progress at Universal Florida than at Disney-MGM. On any day, production crews will be shooting on the Universal backlot in full view of guests who care to watch.

Universal Studios Florida is about twice as large as Disney-MGM, and because almost all of it is open to the public, most of the crowding and congestion so familiar in the streets and plazas of Disney-MGM is eliminated. Universal Studios Florida has plenty of elbow room.

Attractions are excellent at both parks, though Disney-MGM attractions are on average engineered to move people more efficiently. Each park offers a stellar attraction that breaks new ground, transcending in power, originality, and technology any prior standard for theme park entertainment. Universal offers *Terminator 2: 3-D,* which we consider the most extraordinary attraction in any American theme park. Disney-MGM Studios features *The Twilight Zone* Tower of Terror, our pick for the nation's second best attraction. The next best attractions in each park are also well matched: Back to the Future at Universal in a dead heat with Star Tours at Disney-MGM.

Though Universal Studios must be credited with pioneering a number of innovative and technologically advanced rides, it also must be pointed out that Universal's attractions break down more often than Disney-MGM's. Jaws and Kongfrontation, in particular, are notorious for frequent breakdowns.

Amazingly, and to the visitor's advantage, each park offers a completely different product mix, so there is little or no redundancy for a person who visits both. Disney-MGM and Universal Studios Florida each provide good exposure to the cinematic arts, though Universal's presentations are generally more informative and comprehensive. Disney-MGM had a distinct edge in educational content until recently, when it turned several of its better tours into infomercials for Disney films. At Universal, you can still learn about post-production, soundstages, set creation, special effects, directing, and cinematography without being bludgeoned by promotional hype.

Stunt shows are similar at both parks. Disney's *Indiana Jones Epic Stunt Spectacular* and Universal's *The Wild, Wild, Wild West Stunt*

Show are both staged in 2,000-seat stadiums that allow a good view of the action. The *Dynamite Nights Stuntacular* at Universal is staged in the large lagoon, with patrons taking up viewing positions along the railing. The lagoon provides a realistic setting but is so large that the action sometimes is hard to see or follow. All three shows have their moments, and the two stadium shows are fairly informative. In the final analysis, Disney-MGM wins for drama and intensity, while Universal Studios gets the call for variety.

We recommend you try one of the studios. If you enjoy one, you probably will enjoy the other. If you have to choose between them, consider:

1. Touring Time   If you tour efficiently, it takes about seven to eight hours to see Disney-MGM Studios (including a lunch break). Because Universal Studios Florida is larger and contains more (and often less efficiently engineered) rides and shows, touring, including one meal, takes about 9 to 11 hours.

2. Convenience   If you're lodging along International Drive, I-4's northeast corridor, the Orange Blossom Trail (US 441), or in Orlando, Universal Florida is closer. If you're lodging along US 27, FL 192, or in Kissimmee or Walt Disney World, Disney-MGM Studios is more convenient.

3. Endurance   Universal Studios Florida is larger and requires more walking than Disney-MGM, but it is also much less congested, so the walking is easier. Both parks offer wheelchairs and disabled access.

4. Cost   Both parks cost about the same for one-day admission, food, and incidentals. All attractions are included in the admission price. If you go for two days, however, check to see if Universal Studios is running its Second-Day-Free promotion. This gives you two days at Universal Studios for the price of one.

5. Best Days to Go   In order, Tuesdays, Mondays, Thursdays, and Wednesdays are best to visit Universal Studios Florida. At Disney-MGM Studios, visit on a day when early entry isn't in effect.

6. When to Arrive   For Disney-MGM, arrive with your ticket in hand 40 minutes before official opening time. For Universal Studios, arrive with your admission already purchased about 50 minutes before official opening time.

7. Young Children   Both Disney-MGM Studios and Universal Studios Florida are relatively adult entertainment offerings. By our reckoning, half the rides and shows at Disney-MGM and about two-thirds at Universal Studios have a significant potential for frightening young children.

8. Food   Food is generally much better at Universal Studios.

GETTING THERE

The Universal Florida complex can be accessed directly from I-4. Once on-site, you will be directed to park in one of two multitiered parking garages. Parking runs $6 for cars and $7 for RVs. Be sure to write down the location of your car before heading for the parks.

ADMISSION PRICES

Universal offers One-Day, Two-Day, Three-Day, and annual passes. Multiday passes allow you to visit both Universal theme parks on the same day, and unused days are good forever. Multiday passes also allow for early entry on select days. Discounts on the Three-Day passes can be obtained by purchasing in advance on the phone with your credit card at (800) 711-0080. All other prices are the same whether you buy your admission at the gate or in advance. Prices shown below include tax.

	Adults (3–9)	Children
One-Day, One Park Pass	$47	$37
Two-Day Escape Pass	$85	$69
Three-Day Escape Pass	$122	$101
Annual Pass	$191	$165

If you want to visit more than one park on a given day, have your park pass and hand stamped when exiting your first park. At the second park use the readmission turnstile, showing your stamped pass and hand.

Combination passes are available: A four-park, seven-day Orlando Flex Ticket allows unlimited entry to Universal Studios, Universal's Islands of Adventure, Sea World, and Wet 'n Wild and costs about $170 for adults and $136 for children (ages three to nine). A five-park, ten-day pass provides unlimited entry to Universal Studios, Universal's Islands of Adventure, SeaWorld,

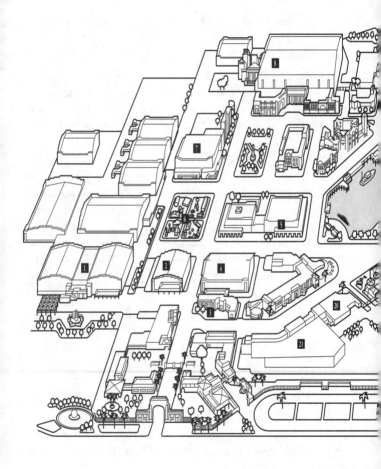

114

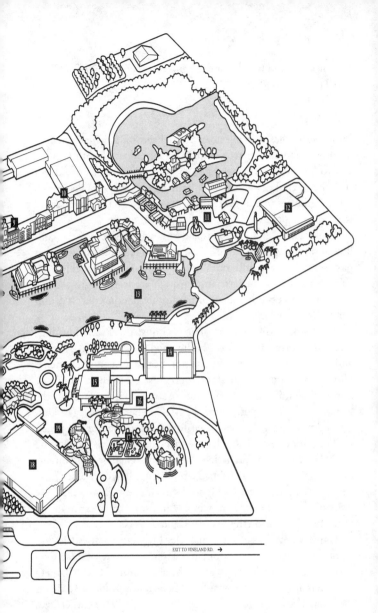

Wet 'n Wild, and Busch Gardens and costs about $209 for adults, and $168 for children.

ARRIVING

From the garages, moving sidewalks deliver you to Universal City-Walk, where you can access the main entrances of both Universal Studios Florida theme park and Universal's Islands of Adventure theme park. Even with the moving walkways it takes about 10–12 minutes to commute from the garages to the entrances of the theme parks.

Universal Studios Florida is laid out in an upside-down L configuration. Beyond the main entrance, a wide boulevard stretches past several shows and rides to a New York City backlot set. Branching off this pedestrian thoroughfare to the right are five streets that access other areas of the studios and intersect a promenade circling a large lake.

The park is divided into five sections: the Front Lot/Production Central, New York, Hollywood, San Francisco/Amity, and Expo Center. Where one section begins and another ends is blurry, but no matter. Guests orient themselves by the major rides, sets, and landmarks and refer, for instance, to "New York," "the waterfront," "over by E.T.," or "by Mel's Diner." The area of Universal Studios Florida open to visitors is about the size of Epcot.

The park offers all standard services and amenities, including stroller and wheelchair rental, lockers, diaper-changing and infant-nursing facilities, car assistance, and foreign-language assistance. Most of the park is accessible to disabled guests, and TDDs are available for the hearing impaired. Almost all services are in the Front Lot, just inside the main entrance.

Universal Studios offers a character breakfast on Tuesdays and Thursdays during slow season, and Monday through Friday during high season. Breakfast is hosted by at least four Hanna-Barbera characters at the International Food Bazaar, just inside the park on the right. The cost is $13.50 for adults and $8.75 for children ages three to nine for an all-you-can-eat cafeteria-style breakfast.

CONTACTING UNIVERSAL FLORIDA

The main Universal Florida information number is (407) 363-8000. Reach Guest Services at (407) 224-6035, schedule a character breakfast at (407) 224-6339, and order tickets by mail at (800) 224-3838.

Universal Studios Florida Attractions

Terminator 2: 3-D

What It Is: 3-D thriller mixed-media presentation

Scope & Scale: Super headliner

When to Go: After 3:30 p.m.

Special Comments: The nation's best theme park attraction; very intense for some preschoolers and grade-schoolers

Author's Rating: Furiously paced high-tech experience; not to be missed; ★★★★★

Overall Appeal by Age Group:

Pre-school	Grade School	Teens	Young Adults	Over 30	Senior Citizens
★★★	★★★★★	★★★★★	★★★★★	★★★★★	★★★★

Duration of Presentation: 20 minutes, including an 8-minute preshow

Probable Waiting Time: 20–40 minutes

Description & Comments   The Terminator "cop" from *Terminator 2* morphs to life and battles Arnold Schwarzenegger's T-800 cyborg character. If you missed the *Terminator* flicks, here's the plot: A bad robot arrives from the future to kill a nice boy. Another bad robot (who has been reprogrammed to be good) pops up at the same time to save the boy. The bad robot chases the boy and the rehabilitated robot, menacing the audience in the process.

The attraction, like the films, is all action, and you really don't need to understand much. What's interesting is that it uses 3-D film and a theater full of sophisticated technology to integrate the real with the imaginary. Images seem to move in and out of the film, not only in the manner of traditional 3-D, but also in actuality. Remove your 3-D glasses momentarily and you'll see that the guy on the motorcycle is actually onstage.

We've watched this type of presentation evolve, pioneered by Disney's *Captain EO, Honey, I Shrunk the Audience,* and

MuppetVision 4D. Terminator 2: 3-D, however, goes way beyond lasers, with moving theater seats, blasts of hot air, and spraying mist. It creates a multidimensional space that blurs the boundary between entertainment and reality. Is it seamless? Not quite, but it's close. We rank *Terminator 2: 3-D* as not to be missed and consider it the absolute best theme-park attraction in the United States. If *Terminator 2: 3-D* is the only attraction you see at Universal Studios Florida, you'll have received your money's worth.

Touring Tips   The 700-seat theater changes audiences about every 19 minutes. Even so, because the show is new and hot, expect to wait about 30–45 minutes. The attraction, on Hollywood Boulevard near the park's entrance, receives huge traffic during morning and early afternoon. By about 3 p.m., however, lines diminish somewhat. Though you'll still wait, we recommend holding off on *Terminator 2: 3-D* until then. If you can't stay until late afternoon, see the show first thing in the morning. Families with young children should know that the violence characteristic of the *Terminator* movies is largely absent from the attraction. There's suspense and action but not much blood and guts.

The Funtastic World of Hanna-Barbera

What It Is: Flight-simulation ride
Scope & Scale: Major attraction
When to Go: Before 11 a.m.
Special Comments: Very intense for some preschoolers
Author's Rating: A delight for all ages; ★★★½
Overall Appeal by Age Group:

Pre-school	Grade School	Teens	Young Adults	Over 30	Senior Citizens
★★★★	★★★★	★★★½	★★★½	★★★½	★★★½

Duration of Ride: 4½ minutes with a 3½-minute preshow
Loading Speed: Moderate to slow

Description & Comments   A flight-simulation ride in the same family as Disney's Star Tours and Body Wars, except that all visuals are cartoons. Guests accompany Yogi Bear in a high-speed chase to rescue a kidnapped child.

Touring Tips   Unfortunately, this wild, funny, and thoroughly delightful attraction is a cycle ride. It must shut down completely during loading and unloading. Consequently, large lines build early and move very slowly. Ride during the first two hours the park is open.

"Alfred Hitchcock: The Art of Making Movies"

What It Is: Mini-course on filming action sequences and a testimonial to the talents of Alfred Hitchcock

Scope & Scale: Major attraction

When to Go: After 3:30 p.m.

Special Comments: May frighten young children

Author's Rating: A little slow-moving, but well done; ★★★½

Overall Appeal by Age Group:

Pre-school	Grade School	Teens	Young Adults	Over 30	Senior Citizens
★★½	★★★	★★★½	★★★½	★★★½	★★★½

Duration of Presentation: 40 minutes

Probable Waiting Time: 22 minutes

Description & Comments   Guests view a film featuring famous scenes from Hitchcock movies (including some unreleased 3-D footage) and then go to an adjoining soundstage where the stabbing scene from *Psycho* is re-created using professional actors and audience volunteers. In a third area, the technology of filming action scenes is explained. The Hitchcock "greatest hits" film is disjointed and confusing unless you have a good recollection of the movies and scenes highlighted. Re-enactment of the scene from *Psycho* is both informative and entertaining, as are sets and techniques demonstrated in the third area.

Touring Tips   The attraction is just beyond the main entrance, and lines build. Usually, however, they disappear quickly. Let morning crowds clear; see the attraction just before you leave in the evening.

Nickelodeon Studios Walking Tour

What It Is: Behind-the-scenes guided tour

Scope & Scale: Minor attraction

When to Go: When Nickelodeon shows are in production (usually weekdays)

Author's Rating: ★★★

Overall Appeal by Age Group:

Pre-school	Grade School	Teens	Young Adults	Over 30	Senior Citizens
★★½	★★★★	★★★	★★★	★★★	★★★

Duration of Tour: 36 minutes
Probable Waiting Time: 30–45 minutes

Description & Comments   The tour examines set construction, soundstages, wardrobe, props, lighting, video production, and special effects. Much of this information is presented more creatively in the "Alfred Hitchcock," *Hercules and Xena,* and *Horror Make-Up Show* productions, but the Nickelodeon tour is tailored for kids. They're made to feel supremely important; their opinions are used to shape future Nickelodeon programming.

Adding some much-needed zip is the Game Lab, where guests preview strange games being tested for possible inclusion on Nickelodeon. Game Lab ends with a lucky child getting "slimed." If you don't understand, consult your children.

Touring Tips   While grade-schoolers, especially, enjoy this tour, it's expendable for everyone else. Go on a second day or second visit at Universal. If Nickelodeon isn't in production, forget it.

Twister

What It Is: Theater presentation featuring special effects from the movie Twister
Scope & Scale: Major attraction
When to Go: Should be your first show after experiencing all rides
Special Comments: High potential for frightening young children
Author's Rating: Gusty; ★★★½

Overall Appeal by Age Group:

Pre-school	Grade School	Teens	Young Adults	Over 30	Senior Citizens
★★	★★★★	★★★★	★★★★	★★★★	★★★★

Duration of Presentation: 15 minutes
Probable Waiting Time: 26 minutes

Description & Comments   Replacing the *Ghostbusters* attraction in 1998, *Twister* combines an elaborate set and special effects, climaxing with a five-story-tall simulated tornado created by circulating more than 2 million cubic feet of air per minute.

Touring Tips The wind, pounding rain, and freight-train sound of the tornado are deafening, and the entire presentation is exceptionally intense. Schoolchildren are mightily impressed, while younger children are terrified and overwhelmed. Unless you want the kids hopping in your bed whenever they hear thunder, try this attraction yourself before taking your kids.

Kongfrontation

What It Is: Indoor adventure ride featuring King Kong

Scope & Scale: Major attraction

When to Go: Before 11 a.m.

Special Comments: May frighten young children

Author's Rating: ★★★★

Overall Appeal by Age Group:

Pre-school	Grade School	Teens	Young Adults	Over 30	Senior Citizens
★★★½	★★★★	★★★½	★★★½	★★★	★★★

Duration of Ride: 4½ minutes

Loading Speed: Moderate

Description & Comments Guests board an aerial tram to ride from Manhattan to Roosevelt Island. En route, they hear the giant ape has escaped. The tram passes evidence of Kong's path of destruction and encounters the monster himself. In the course of the journey, King Kong demolishes buildings, uproots utility poles, swats helicopters, and hurls your tram car to the ground.

Touring Tips A lot of fun when it works. Ride in the morning after Back to the Future, E.T. Adventure, and Jaws.

The Gory Gruesome & Grotesque Horror Make-Up Show

What It Is: Theater presentation on the art of make-up

Scope & Scale: Major attraction

When to Go: After you have experienced all rides

Special Comments: May frighten young children

Author's Rating: A gory knee-slapper; ★★★½

Overall Appeal by Age Group:

Pre-school	Grade School	Teens	Young Adults	Over 30	Senior Citizens
★★★	★★★½	★★★½	★★★½	★★★½	★★★½

Duration of Presentation: 25 minutes

Probable Waiting Time: 20 minutes

Description & Comments   Lively, well-paced look at how make-up artists create film monsters, realistic wounds, severed limbs, and other unmentionables. Funnier and more upbeat than many Universal Studios presentations, the show also presents a wealth of fascinating information. It's excellent and enlightening, if somewhat gory.

Touring Tips   Exceeding most guests' expectations, the *Horror Make-Up Show* is the sleeper attraction at Universal. Its humor and tongue-in-cheek style transcend the gruesome effects, and most folks (including preschoolers) take the blood and guts in stride. It usually isn't too hard to get into.

Hercules and Xena

What It Is: A multisequence course on special effects, mechanical and computer-generated creatures, blue-screen applications, and sound effects

Scope & Scale: Major attraction

When to Go: After you have experienced all the rides

Special Comments: A nice air-conditioned break during the hottest part of the day

Author's Rating: Sugar-coated education; ★★★★

Overall Appeal by Age Group:

Pre-school	Grade School	Teens	Young Adults	Over 30	Senior Citizens
★★★½	★★★★	★★★★	★★★★	★★★★	★★★★

Duration of Presentation: 40 minutes

Probable Waiting Time: 20 minutes

Description & Comments   Guests move from theater to theater in this mini-course attraction. The presentation begins with a preshow that introduces the characters of Hercules and Xena. Next is the Creature Shop, a theater where members of the audience help to create a scene for a Hercules and Xena film by manipulating the limbs of mechanical critters. In the second theater, computer-created special effects are added to the mechanical critters scene and combined through blue-screen technology with backgrounds and footage of the characters Hercules and Xena. In the last theater, sound effects are added to complete the scene.

Touring Tips Informative, worthwhile, sometimes hilarious, and consistently high-tech, *Hercules and Xena* does a great job of making several complicated subjects understandable. The show borrows from the truly amazing technology developed for *Terminator 2: 3-D* and is a more lively presentation than "Murder, She Wrote," which covered much of the same territory. We recommend enjoying the show during the heat of the day.

Earthquake—The Big One

What It Is: Combination theater presentation and adventure ride
Scope & Scale: Major attraction
When to Go: In the morning, after Kongfrontation
Special Comments: May frighten young children
Author's Rating: Not to be missed; ★★★★
Overall Appeal by Age Group:

Pre-school	Grade School	Teens	Young Adults	Over 30	Senior Citizens
★★★	★★★★	★★★★	★★★★	★★★★	★★★★

Duration of Presentation: 20 minutes
Loading Speed: Moderate

Description & Comments Film shows how miniatures are used to create special effects in earthquake movies, followed by a demonstration of how miniatures, blue screen, and matte painting are integrated with live-action stunt sequences (starring audience volunteers) to create a realistic final product. Afterward, guests board a subway from Oakland to San Francisco and experience an earthquake—the big one. Special effects range from fires and runaway trains to exploding tanker trucks and tidal waves. This is Universal's answer to Disney-MGM's Catastrophe Canyon. The special effects are comparable, but the field of vision is better at Catastrophe Canyon. Nonetheless, Earthquake is one of Universal's more compelling efforts.

Touring Tips   Experience Earthquake in the morning, after you ride Back to the Future, E.T., Jaws, and Kongfrontation.

Jaws

What It Is: Adventure boat ride

Scope & Scale: Headliner

When to Go: Before 11 a.m.

Special Comments: Will frighten young children

Author's Rating: Not to be missed; ★★★★

Overall Appeal by Age Group:

Pre-school	Grade School	Teens	Young Adults	Over 30	Senior Citizens
★★½	★★★★	★★★★	★★★★	★★★★	★★★★

Duration of Ride: 5 minutes

Loading Speed: Fast

Probable Waiting Time Per 100 People Ahead of You: 3 minutes

Assumes: All 8 boats are running

Description & Comments   Jaws delivers five minutes of nonstop action, with the huge shark repeatedly attacking. A West Virginia woman, fresh from the Magic Kingdom, told us the shark is "about as pesky as that witch in Snow White." While the story is entirely predictable, the shark is realistic and as big as Rush Limbaugh.

What makes the ride unique is its sense of journey. Jaws builds an amazing degree of suspense. It isn't just a cruise into the middle of a pond where a rubber fish assaults the boat interminably. Add inventive sets and powerful special effects, and you have a first-rate attraction.

A variable at Jaws is the enthusiasm and acting ability of your boat guide. Throughout the ride, the guide must set the tone, elaborate the plot, drive the boat, and fight the shark. Most guides are quite good. They may overact a bit, but you can't fault them for lack of enthusiasm. Consider also that each guide repeats this wrenching ordeal every eight minutes.

Touring Tips   Jaws is as well designed to handle crowds as any theme park attraction in Florida. People on the boat's left side tend to get splashed more.

Back to the Future—The Ride

What It Is: Flight-simulator thrill ride

Scope & Scale: Super headliner

When to Go: First thing in the morning

Special Comments: Very rough ride; may induce motion sickness. Must be 3'4" tall to ride.

Author's Rating: Not to be missed, if you have a strong stomach;
★★★★★

Overall Appeal by Age Group:

Pre-school	Grade School	Teens	Young Adults	Over 30	Senior Citizens
†	★★★★★	★★★★★	★★★★★	★★★★	★★½

† Sample size too small for an accurate rating

Duration of Ride: 4½ minutes

Loading Speed: Moderate

Description & Comments   This attraction is to Universal Studios Florida what Space Mountain is to the Magic Kingdom: the most popular thrill ride in the park. Guests in Doc Brown's lab get caught up in a high-speed chase through time that spans a million years. An extremely intense simulator ride, Back to the Future is similar to Star Tours and Body Wars at Walt Disney World but is much rougher and more jerky. Though the story doesn't make much sense, the visual effects are wild and powerful. The vehicles (Delorean time machines) in Back to the Future are much smaller than those of Star Tours and Body Wars, so the ride feels more personal and less like a group experience.

In a survey of 84 tourists who had experienced simulator rides in both Universal Studios and Disney World, riders younger than 35 preferred Back to the Future to the Disney attractions by a seven-to-four margin. Older riders, however, stated a two-to-one preference for Star Tours over Back to the Future or Body Wars.

Touring Tips   As soon the park opens, guests stampede to Back to the Future. Our recommendation: Be there when the park opens, and join the rush. If you don't ride before 10 a.m., your wait may be exceptionally long. *Note:* Sitting in the rear seat of the car makes the ride more realistic.

E.T. Adventure

What It Is: Indoor adventure ride based on the E.T. movie

Scope & Scale: Major attraction

When to Go: Before 10 a.m.

Author's Rating: ★★★★

Overall Appeal by Age Group:

Pre-school	Grade School	Teens	Young Adults	Over 30	Senior Citizens
★★★★	★★★★	★★★½	★★★½	★★★½	★★★½

Duration of Ride: 4½ minutes

Load Speed: Moderate

Description & Comments   Guests aboard a bicycle-like conveyance escape with E.T. from earthly law enforcement officials and then journey to E.T.'s home planet. The attraction is similar to Peter Pan's Flight at the Magic Kingdom but is longer and has more elaborate special effects and a wilder ride.

Touring Tips   Most preschoolers and grade-school children love E.T. We think it worth a 20- to 30-minute wait, but nothing longer. Lines build quickly after 9:45 a.m., and waits can be more than two hours on busy days. Ride in the morning, right after Back to the Future. Guests who balk at sitting on the bicycle can ride in a comfortable gondola.

Woody Woodpecker's KidZone

What It Is: Interactive playground and kid's roller coaster

Scope & Scale: Minor attraction

When to Go: Anytime

Author's Rating: A good place to let off steam; ★★★

Overall Appeal by Age Group:

Pre-school	Grade School	Teens	Young Adults	Over 30	Senior Citizens
★★★★	★★★	—	—	—	—

Description & Comments   Rounding out the selection of other nearby kid-friendly attractions, the KidZone consists of Woody Woodpecker's Nuthouse Coaster and an interactive playground called Curious George Goes to Town. The child-sized roller coaster is small enough for kids to enjoy but sturdy enough for adults, though its moderate speed might unnerve some smaller children (the minimum age to ride is three years old). The Curious George playground exemplifies the Universal obsession with wet stuff: in addition to innumerable spigots, pipes, and spray guns, two giant roof-mounted buckets periodically dump a thousand gallons of water on unsuspecting visitors below. Kids who want to stay dry can mess around in the foam-ball playground, also equipped with chutes, tubes, and ball-blasters.

Touring Tips Universal employees have already dubbed this new children's area "Peckerland." Visit the playground after you've experienced all the major attractions.

Animal Actors Stage

What It Is: Trained-animals stadium performance

Scope & Scale: Major attraction

When to Go: After you have experienced all rides

Author's Rating: Warm and delightful; ★★★½

Overall Appeal by Age Group:

Pre-school	Grade School	Teens	Young Adults	Over 30	Senior Citizens
★★★★½	★★★★	★★★½	★★★½	★★★½	★★★½

Duration of Presentation: 20 minutes

Probable Waiting Time: 25 minutes

Description & Comments Humorous demonstration of how animals are trained for films. Well-paced and informative, the show features cats, dogs, monkeys, birds, and other creatures. Sometimes animals don't behave as expected, but that's half the fun. Often the animal stars are quite famous. In 1998, for example, a pig from the acclaimed movie *Babe* was featured.

Touring Tips We would like this show better if guests could simply walk in and sit down. As it is, everyone must line up to be admitted. Presented six to ten times daily, the program's schedule is in the daily entertainment guide. Go when it's convenient for you; queue about 15 minutes before show time.

Dynamite Nights Stuntacular

What It Is: Simulated stunt-scene filming

Scope & Scale: Major attraction

When to Go: In the evening according to the daily entertainment schedule

Author's Rating: Well done; ★★★★
Overall Appeal by Age Group:

Pre-school	Grade School	Teens	Young Adults	Over 30	Senior Citizens
★★★	★★★★	★★★★	★★★★	★★★½	★★★½

Duration of Presentation: 20 minutes
Probable Waiting Time: None

Description & Comments   Each evening on the lagoon, stunt men demonstrate spectacular stunts and special effects. The plot involves lawmen trying to intercept and apprehend drug smugglers. Our main problem with this show is that the lagoon is so large that it's somewhat difficult to follow the action. The production was upgraded in 1994 and 1997.

Touring Tips   This version is on a par with Disney-MGM's stunt show. Onlookers watch from the rail encircling the lagoon. There's no waiting in line, but if you want a really good vantage point, stake out your position about 25 minutes before show time. The best viewing spots are along the docks at Lombard's Landing and adjacent areas on the Embarcadero waterfront, across the street from Earthquake. Primary viewing spots are identified on the park map with a "PV" icon.

The Wild, Wild, Wild West Stunt Show

What It Is: Stunt show with a western theme
Scope & Scale: Major attraction
When to Go: After you've experienced all rides
Author's Rating: Solid and exciting; ★★★★
Overall Appeal by Age Group:

Pre-school	Grade School	Teens	Young Adults	Over 30	Senior Citizens
★★★★½	★★★★	★★★★	★★★★	★★★★	★★★★

Duration of Presentation: 16 minutes
Probable Waiting Time: None

Description & Comments   The *Wild West* stunt show has shootouts, fistfights, horse tricks, and high falls, all exciting and well executed. The fast-paced show is staged about ten times daily in a 2,000-seat, covered stadium. Unlike the stunt show on the lagoon, the action is easy to follow.

Touring Tips Show times are listed in the daily entertainment guide; go at your convenience. During summer, the stadium is more comfortable after dusk.

Fievel's Playland

What It Is: Children's play area with water slide

Scope & Scale: Minor attraction

When to Go: Anytime

Author's Rating: A much-needed attraction for preschoolers; ★★★★

Overall Appeal by Age Group:

Pre-school	Grade School	Teens	Young Adults	Over 30	Senior Citizens
★★★★	★★★★	★★★	★★★	★★★	★★★

Probable Waiting Time: 20–30 minutes for the water slide; otherwise, no waiting

Description & Comments Imaginative playground features ordinary household items reproduced on a giant scale, as a mouse would experience them. Preschoolers and grade-schoolers can climb nets, walk through a huge boot, splash in a sardine-can fountain, seesaw on huge spoons, and climb onto a cow skull. Most of the playground is reserved for preschoolers, but a water slide/raft ride is open to all ages.

Touring Tips Walk into Fievel's Playland without waiting, and stay as long as you want. Younger children love the oversized items, and there's enough to keep teens and adults busy while little ones let off steam. The water slide/raft ride is open to everyone but is extremely slow-loading and carries only 300 riders per hour. With the wait an average of 20–30 minutes, we don't think the 16-second ride is worth the trouble. Also, you're highly likely to get soaked.

Lack of shade is a major shortcoming of the entire attraction. Don't go during the heat of the day.

Beetlejuice's Rock 'n Roll Graveyard Revue

What It Is: Rock-and-roll stage show

Scope & Scale: Minor attraction

When to Go: At your convenience

Author's Rating: Outrageous; ★★★½

Overall Appeal by Age Group:

Pre-school	Grade School	Teens	Young Adults	Over 30	Senior Citizens
★★★★	★★★★	★★★★	★★★½	★★★½	★★★½

Duration of Presentation: 16 minutes

Probable Waiting Time: None

Description & Comments   High-powered rock-and-roll stage show stars Beetlejuice, Frankenstein, the Bride of Frankenstein, Wolfman, Dracula, and the Phantom of the Opera. In addition to fine vintage rock, the show features some of the most exuberant choreography found anywhere, plus impressive sets and special effects.

Touring Tips   Mercifully, this attraction has been moved under cover.

A Day in the Park with Barney

What It Is: Live character stage show

Scope & Scale: Major children's attraction

When to Go: Anytime

Author's Rating: A great hit with preschoolers; ★★★★

Overall Appeal by Age Group:

Pre-school	Grade School	Teens	Young Adults	Over 30	Senior Citizens
★★★★½	★★★	★★	★★½	★★★	★★★

Duration of Presentation: 12 minutes plus character greeting

Probable Waiting Time: 15 minutes

Description & Comments   Barney, the purple dinosaur of Public Television fame, leads a sing-along with the help of the audience and sidekicks Baby Bop and BJ. A short preshow gets the kids lathered up before they enter the theater, Barney's Park. Interesting theatrical effects include wind, falling leaves, clouds and stars in the simulated sky, and snow. After the show, Barney exits momentarily to allow parents and children to gather along the stage. He then thunders back and moves from child to child, hugging each and posing for photos.

Touring Tips   If your child likes Barney, this show is a must. It's happy and upbeat, and the character greeting that follows is the best organized we've seen in any theme park. There's no line and no fighting for Barney's attention. Just relax by the rail and await your hug.

Lucy, a Tribute

What It Is: Walk-through tribute to Lucille Ball

Scope & Scale: Diversion

When to Go: Anytime

Author's Rating: A touching remembrance; ★★★

Overall Appeal by Age Group:

Pre-school	Grade School	Teens	Young Adults	Over 30	Senior Citizens
★	★	★★	★★★	★★★	★★★

Probable Waiting Time: None

Description & Comments The life and career of comedienne Lucille Ball are spotlighted, with emphasis on her role as Lucy Ricardo in the long-running television series *I Love Lucy.* Well designed and informative, the exhibit succeeds admirably in recalling the talent and temperament of the beloved redhead.

Touring Tips See Lucy during the hot, crowded midafternoon, or on your way out of the park. Adults could easily stay 15–30 minutes. Children, however, get restless after a couple of minutes.

Street Scenes

What It Is: Elaborate outdoor sets for making films

Scope & Scale: Diversion

When to Go: Anytime

Special Comments: You'll see most sets without special effort as you tour the park

Author's Rating: One of the park's great assets; ★★★★★

Overall Appeal by Age Group:

Pre-school	Grade School	Teens	Young Adults	Over 30	Senior Citizens
★★★	★★★★½	★★★★½	★★★★½	★★★★★	★★★★★

Probable Waiting Time: No waiting

Description & Comments Unlike at Disney-MGM Studios, all Universal Studios Florida's backlot sets are accessible for guest inspection. They include New York City streets, San Francisco's waterfront, a New England coastal town, the house from *Psycho,* Rodeo Drive and Hollywood Boulevard, and a Louisiana bayou.

Touring Tips   You'll see most as you walk through the park.

Universal's Islands of Adventure

When Universal's Islands of Adventure theme park opened in 1999, it provided Universal with enough critical mass to actually compete with Disney. For the first time, Universal has an on-site hotel, a shopping and entertainment complex, and two major theme parks. Doubly interesting is that the new Universal park is pretty much just for fun, in other words, a direct competitor to Disney's Magic Kingdom, the most visited theme park in the world.

How direct a competitor is it? Check this out:

Islands of Adventure	**Magic Kingdom**
Six Islands (includes Port of Entry)	Seven Lands (includes Main Street)
Two roller coasters	Two roller coasters
A Dumbo-type ride	Dumbo
One flume ride	One flume ride
Toon Lagoon character area	Mickey's Toontown Fair character area

And though it may take central Florida tourists awhile to make the connection, here's what will dawn on them when they finally do: Universal's Islands of Adventure is a brand-new, state-of-the-art park competing with a Disney park that is more than 25 years old and has not added a major new attraction for four years.

Of course, that's only how it looks on paper. The reality, as they say, is still blowing in the wind. The Magic Kingdom, after all, is graceful in its maturity and much beloved. And then there was the question on everyone's mind: could Universal really pull it off? Recalling the disastrous first year that the Universal Studios Florida park experienced, we held our breath to see if Islands of Adventure's innovative, high-tech attractions would work. Well, not only did they work, they were up and running almost two months ahead of schedule. Thus, the clash of the titans is once again hot. Universal is coming on strong with the potential of sucking up three days of a tourist's week (more, if you include Universal's strategic relationship with Sea World and Busch Gardens). And that's more time than anyone has spent off the Disney campus for a long, long time.

Through it all, Disney and Universal spokesmen downplayed their fierce competition, pointing out that any new theme park makes central Florida a more marketable destination. Behind closed doors, however, it's a Pepsi/Coke–type rivalry that will undoubtedly keep both companies working hard to gain a competitive edge. The good news, of course, is that this competition translates into better and better attractions for you to enjoy.

BEWARE OF THE WET AND THE WILD

Although we have described Universal's Islands of Adventure as a direct competitor to the Magic Kingdom, there is one major qualification you should be aware of. Whereas most Magic Kingdom attractions are designed to be enjoyed by guests of any age, attractions at Islands of Adventure are largely created for an under-40 population. The roller coasters at Universal are serious with a capital "S," making Space Mountain and Big Thunder Mountain look about as tough as Dumbo. In fact, seven out of the nine top attractions at Islands are thrill rides, and of these, there are three that not only scare the bejeezus out of you but also drench you with water.

In addition to thrill seekers, families with young children will find a lot to do at Islands of Adventure. There are three interactive playgrounds, as well as four rides that young children will enjoy. Of the thrill rides, only the two in Toon Lagoon (described later) are marginally appropriate for young children, and even on these rides your child needs to be fairly stalwart.

ARRIVING

Both Universal theme parks are accessed via the Universal City-Walk entertainment complex. Crossing CityWalk from the parking garages, bear left to Universal's Islands of Adventure.

Universal's Islands of Adventure is arranged much like the World Showcase section of Epcot, in a large circle surrounding a lake. Unlike Epcot, however, the Islands of Adventure theme areas evidence the sort of thematic continuity pioneered by Disneyland and the Magic Kingdom. Each land, or island in this case, is

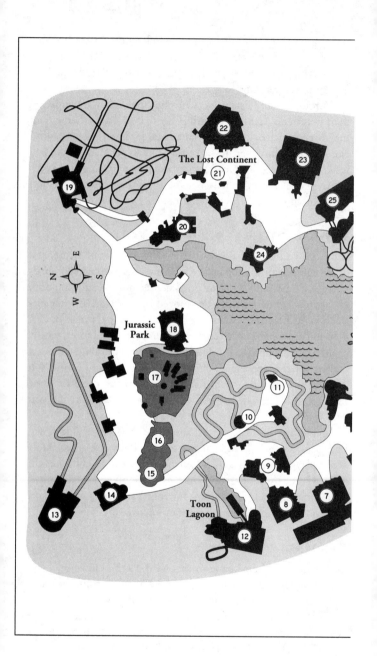

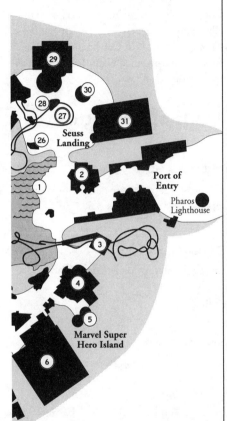

Islands of Adventure

Port of Entry
1. Island Skipper Tours
2. Confisco's Grill

Marvel Super Hero Island
3. Incredible Hulk Coaster
4. Cafe 4
5. Dr. Doom's Fearfall
6. The Amazing Adventure of Spider-Man

Toon Lagoon
7. Pandemonium Cartoon Circus
8. Comic Strip Café
9. Comic Strip Lane
10. Popeye & Bluto's Bilge-Rat Barges
11. Me Ship, *The Olive*
12. Dudley Do-Right's Ripsaw Falls

Jurassic Park
13. Jurassic Park River Adventure
14. Thunder Falls Terrace
15. Camp Jurassic
16. Pteranodon Flyers
17. Triceratops Encounter
18. Jurassic Park Discovery Center

The Lost Continent
19. Dueling Dragons
20. The Enchanted Oak Tavern (and Alchemy Bar)
21. Sinbad's Village
22. *The Eighth Voyage of Sinbad*
23. *Poseidon's Fury! Escape from the Lost City*
24. Mythos Restaurant

Seuss Landing
25. Sylvester McMonkey McBean
26. If I Ran the Zoo
27. Caro-Seuss-El
28. The Once-ler's House
29. Circus McGurkus Cafe Stoo-pendous
30. One Fish Two Fish Red Fish Blue Fish
31. The Cat in the Hat

Pharos Lighthouse

Port of Entry

Seuss Landing

Marvel Super Hero Island

self-contained and visually consistent in its theme, though you can see parts of the other islands across the lake.

Passing through the turnstiles, you first encounter the Moroccan-style Port of Entry, where you will find Guest Services, lockers, stroller and wheelchair rentals, ATM banking, lost and found, and, of course, shopping. From the Port of Entry, moving clockwise around the lake, you can access Marvel Super Hero Island, Toon Lagoon, Jurassic Park, the Lost Continent, and Seuss Landing. You can crisscross the lake on small boats, but otherwise there is no in-park transportation.

Universal's Islands of Adventure Attractions

MARVEL SUPER HERO ISLAND

This island, with its futuristic and retro-future design, and comic book signage, offers shopping and attractions based on Marvel Comic characters.

The Adventures of Spider-Man

What It Is: Indoor adventure simulator ride based on Spider-Man

Scope & Scale: Super headliner

When to Go: Before 10 a.m.

Author's Rating: Our choice for the best attraction in the park; ★★★★★

Overall Appeal by Age Group:

Pre-school	Grade School	Teens	Young Adults	Over 30	Senior Citizens
★★★	★★★★★	★★★★★	★★★★★	★★★★★	★★★★

Duration of Ride: 4½ minutes

Loading Speed: Fast

Description & Comments   Covering 1½ acres and combining moving ride vehicles, 3-D film, and live action, Spider-Man is frenetic, fluid, and astounding. The visuals are rich and the ride is wild, but not jerky. Although the attractions are not directly comparable, Spider-Man is technologically on a par with Disney-

MGM's Tower of Terror, which is to say that it will leave you in awe. As a personal aside, we love both and would be hard-pressed to choose one over the other.

The story line is that you are a reporter for the *Daily Bugle* newspaper (where Peter Parker, a.k.a. Spider-Man, works as a mild-mannered photographer), when it's discovered that evil villains have stolen (I promise I'm not making this up) the Statue of Liberty. You are drafted on the spot by your cantankerous editor to go get the story. After speeding around and being thrust into "a battle between good and evil," you experience a "sensory drop" of 400 feet into darkness. Because the ride is so wild and the action so continuous, it's hard to understand the plot, but you're so thoroughly entertained that you don't really care. Plus, you'll want to ride again and again. Eventually, with repetition, the story line will begin to make sense.

Touring Tips   Ride first thing in the morning after Dr. Doom's FearFall and The Incredible Hulk Coaster, or in the hour before closing.

The Incredible Hulk Coaster

What It Is: Roller coaster

Scope & Scale: Super Headliner

When to Go: Before 9:30 a.m.

Author's Rating: A coaster lover's coaster; ★★★★½

Overall Appeal by Age Group:

Pre-school	Grade School	Teens	Young Adults	Over 30	Senior Citizens
½	★★★★★	★★★★★	★★★★★	★★★★	★★½

Duration of Ride: 1½ minutes

Loading Speed: Moderate

Description & Comments   There is as always a story line, but for this attraction it's of no importance whatsoever. What you need to know about this attraction is simple. You will be launched like a cannonball shot from 0 to 40 miles per hour in two seconds, and then you will be flung upside down 100 feet off the ground, which will, of course, induce weightlessness. From there it's a mere seven rollovers punctuated by two plunges into holes in the ground before you're allowed to get out and throw up.

Seriously, the Hulk is a great roller coaster, perhaps the best in Florida, providing a ride comparable to Montu (Busch Gardens) with the added thrill of an accelerated launch (instead of the more typical uphill crank). Plus, like Montu, the ride is smooth. You won't be jarred and whiplashed on the Incredible Hulk.

Touring Tips   The Hulk gives Spider-Man a run as the park's most popular attraction. Ride early in the morning immediately after Dr. Doom's FearFall. Universal provides electronic lockers near the entrance of the Hulk to deposit any items that might depart your person during the Hulk's seven inversions. Program the number of your locker into the terminal and follow the instructions. You'll receive a slip of paper with a code you can enter when you return to retrieve your stuff. The locker is free if you only use it for a short time. If you leave things in the locker for a couple of hours, however, you'll have to pay a modest rental charge.

Dr. Doom's FearFall

What It Is: Lunch liberator
Scope & Scale: Headliner
When to Go: Before 9:15 a.m.
Author's Rating: More bark than bite; ★★★
Overall Appeal by Age Group:

Pre-school	Grade School	Teens	Young Adults	Over 30	Senior Citizens
—	★★★	★★★★	★★★½	★★★	—

Duration of Ride: 40 seconds
Loading Speed: Slow

Description & Comments   Here you are (again) strapped into a seat with your feet dangling and blasted 200 feet up in the air and then allowed to partially free-fall back down. If you are having trouble forming a mental image of this attraction, picture the midway game where a macho guy swings a sledgehammer, propelling a metal sphere up a vertical shaft. At the top of the shaft is a bell. If the macho man drives the sphere high enough to ring the bell, he wins a prize. Got the idea? OK, on this ride you are the metal sphere.

The good news is this ride looks much worse than it actually is. The scariest part by far is the apprehension that builds as you sit, strapped in, waiting for the thing to launch. The blasting up and free-falling down parts are really very pleasant.

Touring Tips We've seen glaciers that move faster than the line to Dr. Doom. If you want to ride without investing half a day, be one of the first in the park to ride. Fortunately, if you're on hand at opening time, being among the first isn't too difficult (mainly because the nearby Hulk and Spider-Man attractions are bigger draws).

TOON LAGOON

Toon Lagoon is cartoon art translated into real buildings and settings. Whimsical and gaily colored, with rounded and exaggerated lines, Toon Lagoon is Universal's answer to Mickey's Toontown Fair in the Magic Kingdom. The main difference between the two toon lands is that (as you will see) you've about a 60% chance of going into hypothermia at Universal's version.

Dudley Do-Right's Ripsaw Falls

What It Is: Flume ride
Scope & Scale: Headliner
When to Go: Before 10:30 a.m.
Author's Rating: A minimalist Splash Mountain; ★★★½
Overall Appeal by Age Group:

Pre-school	Grade School	Teens	Young Adults	Over 30	Senior Citizens
★★½	★★★★	★★★½	★★★	★★★½	★★½

Duration of Ride: 5 minutes
Loading Speed: Moderate

Description & Comments Inspired by the *Rocky and Bullwinkle* cartoon series, this ride features Canadian Mountie Dudley Do-Right as he attempts to save Nell from evil Snidely Whiplash. Story line aside, it's a flume ride, with the inevitable big drop at the end. Universal claims this is the first flume ride to "send riders plummeting 15 feet below the surface of the water." We're not exactly sure how this works, but it sounds like you better bring your diving gear.

The only problem with this attraction is that everyone inevitably compares it to Splash Mountain at the Magic Kingdom. The flume is as good as Splash Mountain's, and the final drop is a whopper, but the theming and the visuals aren't even in the same league. The art, sets, audio, and jokes at Dudley Do-Right are minimalist at

best, sort of Dudley Do-Right's two-dimensional approach versus
Splash Mountain's three-dimensional presentation. Taken on its
own terms, however, Dudley Do-Right is a darn good flume ride.

Touring Tips   This ride will get you wet, but on average not as
wet as you might expect (it looks worse than it is). If you want
to stay dry, however, arrive prepared with a poncho or at least a
big garbage bag with holes cut out for your head and arms. After
riding, take a moment to gauge the timing of the water cannons
that go off along the exit walk. This is where you can really get
drenched. While younger children are often intimidated by the
big drop, those who ride generally enjoy themselves. Ride first
thing in the morning after experiencing the Marvel Super Hero
rides.

Popeye & Bluto's Bilge-Rat Barges

What It Is: Whitewater raft ride
Scope & Scale: Headliner
When to Go: Before 10:30 a.m.
Author's Rating: Bring your own soap; ★★★★
Overall Appeal by Age Group:

Pre-school	Grade School	Teens	Young Adults	Over 30	Senior Citizens
★★★	★★★★½	★★★★	★★★★	★★★½	★★½

Duration of Ride: 4½ minutes
Loading Speed: Moderate

Description & Comments   This sweetly named attraction is a
whitewater raft ride that includes an encounter with an 18-foot-
tall octopus. Engineered to ensure that everyone gets drenched,
the ride even provides water cannons for highly intelligent non-
participants ashore to fire at those aboard. The rapids are rougher
and more interesting, and the ride longer, than the Animal Kingdom's Kali River Rapids. But nobody surpasses Disney for visuals
and theming, though the settings of these two attractions (cartoon
set and Asian jungle river, respectively) are hardly comparable.

Touring Tips   If you didn't drown on Dudley Do-Right, here's a
second chance. You'll get a lot wetter from the knees down on this
ride, so use your poncho or garbage bag and ride barefoot with
your britches rolled up. In terms of beating the crowds, ride the

barges in the morning after experiencing the Marvel Super Hero attractions and Dudley Do-Right. If you are lacking foul weather gear or forgot your trash bag, you might want to put off riding until last thing before leaving the park. Most preschoolers enjoy the raft ride. Those who are frightened react more to the way the rapids look as opposed to the roughness of the ride.

Me Ship, The Olive

What It Is: Interactive playground

Scope & Scale: Minor attraction

When to Go: Anytime

Author's Rating: Colorful and appealing for kids; ★★★

Overall Appeal by Age Group:

Pre-school	Grade School	Teens	Young Adults	Over 30	Senior Citizens
★★★★	★★★½	½	½	½	—

Description & Comments   *The Olive* is Popeye's three-story boat come to life as an interactive playground. Younger children can scramble around in Swee' Pea's Playpen, while older sibs shoot water cannons at riders trying to survive the adjacent Bilge-Rat raft ride.

Touring Tips   If you are into the big rides, save the playground for later in the day.

Pandemonium Cartoon Circus

What It Is: Musical stage show featuring cartoon characters

Scope & Scale: Headliner

When to Go: After experiencing the rides

Author's Rating: ★★★½

Overall Appeal by Age Group:

Pre-school	Grade School	Teens	Young Adults	Over 30	Senior Citizens
★★★★	★★★½	★★★	★★★	★★★	★★★

Duration of Presentation: 20 minutes

Probable Wait: 15 minutes

Description & Comments   This stage show features seemingly any and every cartoon character whose rights aren't tied up by Disney or Warner Brothers. If you see it with your kids, you'll be busy helping each other identify characters that don't span the generation gap. The show itself is long on enthusiasm and energy. Though competently performed and certainly entertaining, you'll feel like you've been to cheerleading camp by the time it's over.

Touring Tips   The show is staged in a large covered theater that is sometimes taken over by television shows taping on property. Character shows are scheduled about six times daily according to the show times listed in the handout park map. See the show at your convenience after experiencing the rides and seeing *Poseidon's Fury*.

Comic Strip Lane

What It Is: Walk-through exhibit and shopping/dining venue
Scope & Scale: Diversion
When to Go: Anytime

Description & Comments   This is the main street of Toon Lagoon. Here you can visit the domains of Beetle Bailey, Hagar the Horrible, Krazy Kat, the Family Circus, and Blondie and Dagwood, among others. Shops and eateries tie into the cartoon strip theme.

Touring Tips   This is a great place for photo ops with cartoon characters in their own environment. It's also a great place to drop a few bucks in the diners and shops, but you probably already figured that out.

JURASSIC PARK

Jurassic Park (for anyone who's been asleep for 20 years) is a Steven Spielberg film about a fictitious theme park with real dinosaurs. Jurassic Park at Universal's Islands of Adventure is a real theme park (or at least a section of one) with fictitious dinosaurs.

Jurassic Park River Adventure

What It Is: Indoor/outdoor adventure ride based on the *Jurassic Park* movie
Scope & Scale: Super headliner
When to Go: Before 11 a.m.
Author's Rating: Better than it's Hollywood cousin; ★★★★
Overall Appeal by Age Group:

Pre-school	Grade School	Teens	Young Adults	Over 30	Senior Citizens
★★★	★★★★½	★★★★	★★★★	★★★★	★★★½

Duration of Ride: 6½ minutes
Loading Speed: Fast

Description & Comments   Guests board boats for a water tour of Jurassic Park. Everything is tranquil as the tour begins, and the boat floats among large herbivorous dinosaurs such as brontosaurus and stegosaurus. Then, as word is received that some of the carnivores have escaped their enclosure, the tour boat is accidentally diverted into Jurassic Park's maintenance facilities. Here, the boat and its riders are menaced by an assortment of hungry meat eaters led by the ubiquitous T-Rex. At the climactic moment, the boat and its passengers escape by plummeting over an 85-foot drop billed as the "longest, fastest, steepest water descent ever built" (did anyone other than me notice the omission of the word wettest?).

Touring Tips   Though the boats make a huge splash at the bottom of the 85-foot drop, you don't get all that wet. Before the boat leaves the dock, however, you must sit in the puddles left by previous riders. Once underway there's a little splashing, but nothing major until the big drop at the end of the ride. When you hit the bottom, however, enough water will cascade into the air to extinguish a three-alarm fire. Fortunately, not all that much lands in the boat.

Young children must endure a double whammy on this ride. First, they are stalked by giant, salivating (sometimes spitting) reptiles, and then they're sent catapulting over the falls. Unless your children are fairly stalwart, wait a year or two before you spring the River Adventure on them.

Triceratops Encounter

What It Is: Prehistoric petting zoo
Scope & Scale: Minor attraction
When to Go: Before 11:30 a.m.
Author's Rating: Well executed; ★★★
Overall Appeal by Age Group:

Pre-school	Grade School	Teens	Young Adults	Over 30	Senior Citizens
★★★★	★★★★	★★★½	★★★½	★★★½	★★★½

Duration of Show: 5 minutes
Probable Waiting Time: 15–25 minutes

Description & Comments   Guests are ushered in groups into a "feed and control station," where they can view and pet a 24-foot-long, animatronic triceratops dinosaur. While the trainer lectures about the creature's behaviors, habits, and lifestyle, the triceratops breathes, blinks, chews, and flinches at the touch of the guests.

Touring Tips   Nothing is for sure, but this may be the only attraction in the park where you won't get wet. Just to be sure, however, stand near the middle of the dinosaur. Though not a major attraction, Triceratops Encounter is popular and develops long lines. Make it your first show/exhibit after experiencing the rides.

Discovery Center

What It Is: Interactive natural history exhibit
Scope & Scale: Minor attraction
When to Go: Anytime
Author's Rating: ★★★
Overall Appeal by Age Group: Not open to the public at press time

Description & Comments   The Discovery Center is an interactive, educational exhibit that mixes fiction from the movie, such as using fossil DNA to bring dinosaurs to life, with various skeletal remains and other paleontological displays. One exhibit allows guests to watch an animatronic raptor being hatched. Another allows you to digitally "fuse" your DNA with a dinosaur to see what the resultant creature would look like. Other exhibits include dinosaur egg scanning and identification and a quiz call "You Bet Jurassic."

Touring Tips   Cycle back after experiencing all the rides or on a second day. Most folks can digest this exhibit in 10–15 minutes.

Pteranodon Flyers

What It Is: Dinosaur version of Dumbo, the Flying Elephant
Scope & Scale: Minor attraction
When to Go: When there's no line
Author's Rating: All sizzle, no steak; ½
Overall Appeal by Age Group:

Pre-school	Grade School	Teens	Young Adults	Over 30	Senior Citizens
★★★	★★	★	★½	★	★½

Duration of Ride: 1¼ minutes

Loading Speed: Slower than anyone thought possible

Description & Comments This attraction is Islands of Adventure's biggest blunder. Engineered to accommodate only 170 persons per hour (about half the hourly capacity of Dumbo!), the ride swings you along a track that passes over a small part of Jurassic Park. We recommend that you skip this one. Why? Because the Jurassic period will probably end before you reach the front of the line! And your reward for all that waiting? A one minute and fifteen second ride. Plus, the attraction has a name that nobody over 12 years old can pronounce.

Touring Tips Photograph the pteranodon as it flies overhead. You're probably looking at something that will soon be extinct.

Camp Jurassic

What It Is: Interactive play area
Scope & Scale: Minor attraction
When to Go: Anytime
Author's Rating: Creative playground, confusing layout; ★★★
Overall Appeal by Age Group:

Pre-school	Grade School	Teens	Young Adults	Over 30	Senior Citizens
★★★	★★★	—	—	—	—

Description & Comments Camp Jurassic is a great place for children to let off steam. Sort of a Jurassic version of Tom Sawyer Island, kids can explore lava pits, caves, mines, and a rain forest.

Touring Tips Camp Jurassic will fire the imaginations of the under-13 set. If you don't impose a time limit on the exploration, you could be here awhile. The layout of the play area is confusing and intersects the queuing area for the Pteranodon Flyers. If your child accidentally lines up for the Pteranodons, he'll be college age before you see him again.

LOST CONTINENT

This theme area is an exotic mix of Silk Road bazaar and ancient ruins, with Greco-Moroccan accents. And you thought your decorator was nuts. Anyway, this is the land of mythical gods, fabled beasts, and expensive souvenirs.

Poseidon's Fury! Escape from the Lost City

What It Is: High-tech theater attraction

Scope & Scale: Headliner

When to Go: After experiencing all the rides.

Special Comments: Audience stands throughout

Author's Rating: Packs a punch; ★★★★

Overall Appeal by Age Group:

Pre-school	Grade School	Teens	Young Adults	Over 30	Senior Citizens
★★	★★★★	★★★★	★★★★	★★★★	★★★★

Duration of Presentation: 17 minutes including preshow

Probable Waiting Time: 25 minutes

Description & Comments   In this megatheater attraction, Poseidon, the Greek god of the sea, dukes it out with Zeus, the Greek gods' head honcho. All this happens, of course, with you in the middle, but with less subtlety than in the average dysfunctional family quarrel. The operative word in this brawl is special effects. Poseidon fights with water, 350,000 gallons to be specific, while Zeus uses fire.

The plot unravels in installments as you pass through a couple of preshow areas and finally into the main theater. Though the production is a little slow and plodding at first, it wraps up with quite an impressive flourish. The special effects are, well . . . special. There's some great technology at work here. Poseidon is by far and away the best of the Islands of Adventure theater attractions and a close runner-up to *Terminator 2: 3-D* at the Studios.

Touring Tips   If you are still wet from Dudley Do-Right, the Bilge-Rat Barges, and the Jurassic Park River Adventure, you will probably be pulling for Zeus in hopes you might finally dry out. Our money, however, is on Poseidon. It's legal in Florida for theme parks to get you wet, but setting you on fire is somewhat frowned upon.

Frequent explosions and noise may frighten younger children, so exercise caution with preschoolers. Shows run continuously if the technology isn't on the blink. We recommend catching Poseidon after experiencing your fill of the rides.

Dueling Dragons

What It Is: Roller coaster

Scope & Scale: Headliner

When to Go: Before 10:30 a.m.

Author's Rating: Almost as good as the Hulk Coaster; ★★★★

Overall Appeal by Age Group:

Pre-school	Grade School	Teens	Young Adults	Over 30	Senior Citizens
—	★★★★	★★★★	★★★★	★★★★	★★

Duration of Ride: A minute and 45 seconds

Loading Speed: Moderate

Description & Comments This high-tech coaster launches two trains (Fire and Ice) at the same time on tracks that are closely intertwined. Each track, however, is differently configured so that you get a different experience on each. Several times, a collision with the other train seems imminent, a catastrophe that seems all the more real because the coasters are inverted (i.e., suspended from above so that you sit with your feet dangling). At times, the two trains and their passengers are separated by a mere 12 inches.

Because this is an inverted coaster, your view of the action is limited unless you are sitting in the front row. This means that most passengers miss seeing all these near collisions. But don't worry; regardless of where you sit, there's plenty to keep you busy. Dueling Dragons is the highest coaster in the park and also claims the longest drop at 115 feet, not to mention five inversions. And like the Hulk, it's a nice smooth ride all the way.

Coaster cadets are already arguing about which seat on which train provides the wildest ride. We prefer the front row on either train, but coaster loonies hype the front row of Fire and the last row of Ice.

Touring Tips The good news about this ride is that you won't get wet unless you wet yourself. The bad news is that wetting yourself comes pretty naturally. The other bad news is that the queuing area for Dueling Dragons is the longest, most convoluted affair we've ever seen, winding endlessly through a maze of subterranean passages. After what feels like a comprehensive tour of Mammoth

Cave, you finally emerge at the loading area where you must choose between riding Fire or Ice. Of course, at this critical juncture, you're as blind as a mole rat from being in the dark for so long. Our advice is to follow the person in front of you until your eyes adjust to the light. Though the coasters are slightly different, it takes a lot of rides to apprehend the difference. Try to ride during the first 90 minutes the park is open. Finally, warn anyone waiting for you that you might be a while. Even if there is no line to speak of it takes 10–12 minutes just to navigate the caverns and not much less time to exit the attraction after riding.

The Eighth Voyage of Sinbad

What It Is: Theater stunt show

Scope & Scale: Major attraction

When to Go: Anytime as per the daily entertainment schedule

Author's Rating: Not inspiring; ★★

Overall Appeal by Age Group:

Pre- school	Grade School	Teens	Young Adults	Over 30	Senior Citizens
★★★	★★★½	★★½	★★★	★★★	★★½

Duration of Presentation: 17 minutes

Probable Waiting Time: 15 minutes

Description & Comments   A story about Sinbad the Sailor is the glue that (loosely) binds this stunt show featuring water explosions, ten-foot-tall circles of flame, and various other daunting eruptions. The show reminds us of those action genre movies that substitute a mind-numbing succession of explosions, crashes, and special effects for plot and character development. Concerning Sinbad, even if you bear in mind that it's billed as a stunt show, the production is so vacuous and redundant that it's hard to get into the action. Hercules and Xena fans might appreciate the humor more than the average showgoer.

Touring Tips   See Sinbad after you've experienced the rides and the better rated shows. The theater seats 1,700; performance times are listed in the daily entertainment schedule.

SEUSS LANDING

A ten-acre theme area based on Dr. Seuss's famous children's books. Like at Mickey's Toontown in the Magic Kingdom, all of the buildings and attractions replicate a whimsical, brightly colored cartoon style with exaggerated features and rounded lines.

The Cat in the Hat

What It Is: Indoor adventure ride

Scope & Scale: Major attraction

When to Go: Before 11:30 a.m.

Author's Rating: Seuss would be proud; ★★★½

Overall Appeal by Age Group:

Pre-school	Grade School	Teens	Young Adults	Over 30	Senior Citizens
★★★★	★★★★	★★★	★★★½	★★★½	★★★½

Duration of Ride: 3½ minutes

Loading Speed: Moderate

Description & Comments   Guests ride on "couches" through 18 different sets inhabited by animatronic Seuss characters, including The Cat in the Hat, "Thing 1," "Thing 2," and the beleaguered goldfish who tries to maintain order in the midst of mayhem. Well done overall, with nothing that should frighten younger children.

Touring Tips   This should be fun for all ages. Try to ride early.

One Fish, Two Fish, Red Fish, Blue Fish

What It Is: Wet version of Dumbo, the Flying Elephant

Scope & Scale: Minor attraction

When to Go: Before 10 a.m.

Author's Rating: Who says you can't teach an old ride new tricks? ★★★½

Overall Appeal by Age Group:

Pre-school	Grade School	Teens	Young Adults	Over 30	Senior Citizens
★★★★	★★★★	★★★	★★★	★★★	★★★

Duration of Ride: 2 minutes
Loading Speed: Slow

Description & Comments   Imagine Dumbo with Seuss-style fish instead of elephants and you've got half the story. The other half of the story involves yet another opportunity to drown. Guests steer their fish up or down 15 feet in the air while traveling in circles. At the same time, they try to avoid streams of water projected from "squirt posts." A catchy song provides clues for avoiding the squirting.

Though ostensibly a children's ride, the song and the challenge of steering your fish away from the water jets make this attraction fun for all ages.

Touring Tips   We don't know what it is about this theme park and water, but you'll get wetter than at a full-immersion baptism.

Caro-Seuss-El

What It Is: Merry-go-round
Scope & Scale: Minor attraction
When to Go: Before 10:30 a.m.
Author's Rating: Wonderfully unique; ★★★½
Overall Appeal by Age Group:

Pre-school	Grade School	Teens	Young Adults	Over 30	Senior Citizens
★★★★	★★★★	—	—	—	—

Duration of Ride: 2 minutes
Loading Speed: Slow

Description & Comments   Totally outrageous, the Caro-Seuss-El is a full-scale, 56-mount merry-go-round made up exclusively of Dr. Seuss characters.

Touring Tips   Even if you are too old or don't want to ride, this attraction is worth an inspection. Whatever your age, chances are good you'll see some old friends. If you are touring with young children, try to get them on early in the morning.

Sylvester McMonkey McBean's Very Unusual Driving Machines

What It Is: Indoor/outdoor track ride

Scope & Scale: Major attraction
When to Go: Before 10:30 a.m.
Author's Rating: Not open at press time
Overall Appeal by Age Group: Not open at press time
Duration of Ride: 5 minutes
Loading Speed: Slow

Description & Comments   This long-titled ride offers a tour of Seuss Landing on an elevated track, passing in and out of various attractions, shops, and restaurants. The inspiration, a Seuss book about discrimination, is sort of lost in the translation. Guests can, however (within limits), control the speed of their vehicle (conducive to bumping other cars), honk their horns, and shout expletives commonly associated with California freeway driving.

Touring Tips   Visually appealing. You can cover the same territory on foot.

If I Ran the Zoo

What It Is: Interactive playground
Scope & Scale: Minor attraction
When to Go: Anytime
Author's Rating: Eye-catching; ★★★
Overall Appeal by Age Group:

Pre-school	Grade School	Teens	Young Adults	Over 30	Senior Citizens
★★★★	★★★	—	—	—	—

Description & Comments   Based on Dr. Seuss's *If I Ran the Zoo*, the playground is divided into three distinct areas—Hedges, Water, and the New Zoo. Each features interactive elements, including, of course, another opportunity for a good soaking.

Touring Tips   Visit this playground after you've experienced all the major attractions.

Part Seven

Water Parks

Disney Water Parks vs. Wet 'n Wild and Water Mania

Disney's water parks are distinguished more by their genius for creating an integrated adventure environment than by their slides and individual attractions. At the Disney water parks, both eye and body are deluged with the strange, exotic, humorous, and beautiful. Each Disney park is stunningly landscaped. Parking lots, street traffic, and so on are far removed from and out of sight of the swimming areas. Also, each park has its own story to tell, a theme that forms the background for your swimming experience. Once you've passed through the turnstile, you're totally enveloped in a fantasy setting that excludes the outside world.

For many, however, the novelty of the theme is quickly forgotten once they hit the water, and the appreciation of being in an exotic setting gives way to enjoying specific attractions and activities. In other words, your focus narrows from the general atmosphere of the park to the next slide you want to ride. Once this occurs, the most important consideration becomes the quality and number of attractions and activities available and their accessibility relative to crowd conditions. Viewed from this perspective, the non-Disney water parks, especially Wet 'n Wild, give Disney more than a run for the money.

GETTING THERE

Wet 'n Wild Wet 'n Wild is located at 6200 International Drive in Orlando, about two miles from Universal Florida and SeaWorld on International Drive at Universal Boulevard. From I-4, take exit 30-A, and follow the signs to the park.

Water Mania   Water Mania is located at 6073 W. Irlo Bronson Memorial Highway (U.S. 192), a few miles east of the Disney complex in Kissimmee. From the Disney area, take I-4 to Exit 25A, and head east for 1/2 mile. The park is across from Celebration (Disney's residential area), near visitor guide marker #8. Parking is $4 per car.

ADMISSION PRICES

Wet 'n Wild   Wet 'n Wild has daily general admission passes, and annual passes for $80. During the Summer Nights sessions (late June–early August, after 5 p.m.) hours are extended until 11 p.m., a single general admission is $10 off, and Summer Nights passes are $35. You may, of course, stay through Summer Nights' special hours with a general admission pass.

General admission:
Adults: $26.95 (ages 10 and up)
Children: $21.95 (ages 3–9, free for children under 3 years)
Senior Citizens: $13.28

Water Mania   General Admission covers the entire park.

Adults: $25.95
Children: $18.95 (ages 3–9, free for children under 3 years)

ARRIVING

Wet 'n Wild   Wet 'n Wild is open year-round, with seasonal hours. In Winter, the park is open from 10 a.m.–5 p.m.; Spring, from 10 a.m–6 p.m.; Summer, from 9:30 a.m.–8 p.m. (except during Summer Nights, when the park is open until 11 p.m.); and Fall, from 10 a.m.–6 p.m. During colder months, pools are heated.

Tubes, towels, and lockers are available for rent for $4, $2, and $5 respectively (with a $2 deposit for each). They also offer a package deal including all three for $9 ($4 deposit). Life vests are free. You can bring your own floatation devices, but you can only use them once they've passed park standards. In addition, there is a little gift shop on the premesis where you can stock up on sunscreen, film, and other supplies you might have left behind or run out of.

Picnics are allowed, but no glass containers or alcohol are permitted on park grounds.

Water Mania Water Mania is open year-round (children's area pools are heated from November through March), with opening and closing times that vary by season. Generally, Winter hours (December–March) are 11 a.m.–5 p.m.; Spring hours (April and May) are 10 a.m.–5 or 6 p.m.; Summer hours (Memorial Day–August) are 9:30 a.m.–6 or 7 p.m.; and Fall hours (September and October) are 10 or 11 a.m.–5 p.m. Most Summer weekends have extended hours.

As with all the water parks, you can expect a lot of families with young children, so the prime spots for settling in around the park go quickly. Arrive early, and you'll miss the long entrance lines and find room to stake your claim. Tubes are provided at each ride that requires one, but you can save time waiting in line for the freebies by renting your own for a small fee. Life vests are free with a small deposit. You may also bring your own floatation devices, but be aware that with the exception of the children's areas, they must meet Coast Guard standards for you to use them.

As a nice touch, you can bring your own picnic lunch to eat under one of the covered pavilions in the wooded (read: shady) picnic area. No glass or alcohol is allowed. Kokomos, the Water Mania gift shop, also stocks sunscreen and clothing.

CONTACTING THE WATER PARKS

Wet 'n Wild Wet 'n Wild has a 24-hour information line, (800) 992-WILD, or visit their web site at www.wetnwild.com.

Water Mania For more information on Water Mania, call (800) 527-3092 or visit their web site at www.watermania-florida.com.

A Flume-to-Flume Comparison

The following chart will provide a sense of what each park offers. In standard theme park jargon, the water parks refer to their various features, including slides, as "attractions." Some individual attractions consist of several slides. If each slide at a specific attraction is different, we count them separately. Runoff Rapids at Blizzard Beach, for example, offers three corkscrew slides, each somewhat different. Because most guests want to experience all three we count each individually. At the Toboggan Racers attraction (also at Blizzard Beach), there are eight identical slides side by side. Because they're all exactly the same, there's no reason to ride all eight, so we count the whole Toboggan Racers attraction as one slide. Also, because it's not really in the same league, we've eliminated Disney's River Country from the comparison.

Flumes	Blizzard Beach	Typhoon Lagoon	Wet 'n Wild	Water Mania
Vertical Speed Body Slide	1		2	1
Vertical Speed Tube Slide				1
Twisting Body Slide			1	
Camel Hump Body Slide	1	1		1
Camel Hump Mat Slide	2			
Camel Hump Tube Slide			1	
Corkscrew Mat Slide			3	2
Corkscrew Body Slide		3		
Open Corkscrew Tube Slide	3			
Dark Corkscrew Tube Slide	1		1	2
1–3 Person Raft Flume		2	1	
4–5 Person Raft Flume	1	1	2	1
Total Slides	9	7	11	8

Other Attractions	Blizzard Beach	Typhoon Lagoon	Wet 'n Wild	Water Mania
Interactive Water Ride	1	1	1	1
Wave Pool	1		1	1
Surf Pool		1		
Snorkeling Pool		1		
Stationary Surfing Wave				1
Isolated Children's Area	2	2	2	2
Other Attractions Total	4	5	6	6
Total Slides and Attractions	13	12	17	14

Do the numbers tell the story? In the case of Wet 'n Wild they certainly do. If you can live without the Disney theme setting and story line, Wet 'n Wild offers more attractions and more variety than any of the other parks. Plus, throughout the summer, Wet 'n Wild is open until 11 p.m., offering live bands and dancing nightly. Even if you don't care about the bands or dancing, summer nights are more comfortable, lines for the slides are shorter, and you don't have to worry about sunburn.

Generally speaking, during the day, you'll find Water Mania the least crowded of the parks, followed by Wet 'n Wild. The Disney parks quite often sell out by about 11 a.m. This is followed by long waits for all of the slides.

Although not approaching Disney's standard for aesthetic appeal and landscaping, both Wet 'n Wild and Water Mania are clean and attractive. In the surf and wave pool department, Typhoon Lagoon wins hand down. Whereas its surf lagoon produces six-foot waves that you can actually body surf, the wave pools of the other parks offer only "bobbing" action. All of the parks have outstanding water activity areas for younger children, and each park features at least one unique attraction. Wet 'n Wild has an interactive ride where you control your speed and movements with water blasts, Blizzard Beach has a 1,200-foot water bobsled, Water Mania has a surfing wave, and at Typhoon Lagoon you can snorkel among live fish.

Prices for one-day admission are about the same at Blizzard Beach, Typhoon Lagoon, and Wet 'n Wild, and slightly less at Water Mania. Disney's River Country is the least expensive of the water parks, but although great for swimming and sunning, it doesn't offer much in the way of attractions. Discount coupons are often available in free local visitor magazines for Wet 'n Wild and Water Mania.

Part Eight

After Dark

Dinner Theaters

Central Florida probably has more dinner attractions than anywhere else on earth. The name dinner attraction is something of a misnomer, because dinner is rarely the attraction. These are audience-participation shows or events with food served along the way. They range from extravagant productions where guests sit in arenas at long tables, to intimate settings at individual tables. Don't expect terrific food, but if you're looking for something entertaining outside Walt Disney World, consider one of these.

If you decide to try a non-Disney dinner show, scavenge local tourist magazines from brochure racks and hotel desks outside the World. These free publications usually have discount coupons for area shows.

The Shows

Arabian Nights

Address: 6225 West Irlo Bronson Highway, Kissimmee (US 192 just east of I-4)

Phone: (407) 239-9223

Show Times: Nightly at varying times; currently at 7:30 p.m.; one show only

Reservations: Can usually be made through the day of the show

Cost: $36.95; $23.95 ages 3–11

Discounts: Discount coupons in local visitor magazines, AAA, seniors

Type of Seating: Long rows of benches at tables flanking either side of a large riding arena. All seats face the action.

Menu: Minestrone, prime rib, mixed vegetables, new potatoes, and sheet cake. Children's alternative is chicken fingers with mashed potatoes.

Vegetarian Alternative: Lasagna

Beverages: Unlimited beer, wine, tea, coffee, and soft drinks

Description & Comments   Horses and riders present equestrian skills and trick riding with costumes, music, and theatrical lighting. The loose story line involves a princess who spots a handsome prince who then disappears. A genie appears to grant her three wishes, which, of course, she uses to try to find the stud on the steed. For some reason, she doesn't just tell the genie to produce the guy front and center. They travel the world over—and back in time—to look for him. The search takes them anywhere you might find horses: the circus, the Wild West, the set of *Ben Hur*. In all, horses perform to musical accompaniment.

If you are an unbridled horse fan, you're going to think you've died and gone to heaven. Fifty horses, including Lipizzans, palominos, quarter horses, and Arabians, perform 22 acts. The stunts are impressive, and a great deal of skill and timing is employed to pull them off. But after awhile the tricks start to look the same, only the costumes and the music are different. The whole thing ends in a patriotic ploy.

Arabian Nights' food is distinguished in that it's the only dinner-show fare that doesn't include chicken. The prime rib is edible, and the lasagna alternative is fine. The salad is unappealing, as is the dessert.

Medieval Times Dinner & Tournament

Address: 4510 East US Highway 192, Kissimmee

Phone: (800) 229-8300

Show Times: Vary according to season and nights

Reservations: Best to make reservations a week ahead

Cost: $38.95; $23.95 ages 3–12 (does not include tax or tip)

Discounts: Seniors, military, AAA, hotel employees, travel agents. You get free admission on your birthday.

Type of Seating: Arena-style, in rows that face the riding floor

Menu: Vegetable soup, whole roasted chicken, spare ribs, herb-basted potatoes, and strudel. Everything is eaten with the hands; no utensils are provided.

Vegetarian Alternative: Lasagna, or raw veggies with dip plate

Beverages: Two rounds of beer, sangria, or soft drinks; cash bar available

Description & Comments   A tournament set 900 years in the past pits six knights against each other. Audience members are seated in areas corresponding to the color of the knights' pennants and are encouraged to cheer for their knight and to boo his opponents. Part of the tournament is actual competition. The knights perform stunts, including hitting a target with a lance or collecting rings on a lance while riding horseback. After each event, successful knights receive carnations from the queen to toss to young ladies in their sections.

After a while, the tournament takes on a choreographed feel—and with good reason. It comes down to a fight to the finish until only one knight is left standing. There are cheating knights who pull others off their horses and hand-to-hand combat with maces, battle-axes, and swords. The winning knight selects a fair maiden from the audience to be his princess.

The food is remarkable only in that you eat it with your hands, including a whole chicken you must pull apart. The chicken is good, the ribs a little tough. The appetizer (surely you jest) is a hamburger bun, either top or bottom, slathered with tomato sauce and melted cheese. Very cheesy, indeed.

The show is good, and the knights put out 100% (the bruises these guys must get!). The sword fights are so realistic that sparks fly off the metal blades. Audience participation reaches a fever pitch, with each section cheering for its knight and calling for the death of the dastardly opponents. It's amazing how bloodthirsty people can be after they've ripped a chicken apart with their bare hands.

With all the horses, jousting, and fighting, children shouldn't be bored, though parents of very young children might be concerned about the violence.

Capone's Dinner & Show

Address: 4740 West US 192, Kissimmee

Phone: (407) 397-2378

Show Times: 8 p.m. nightly; changes seasonally

Reservations: Need to make reservations several days in advance

Cost: $37; $24 ages 4–12 (does not include tax or tip)

Discounts: Florida residents, AAA, seniors, military, hospitality workers

Type of Seating: Long tables with large groupings facing an elevated stage; some smaller tables for parties of two to six

Menu: Buffet with lasagna, baked ziti, spaghetti, baked chicken, baked ham, boiled potatoes, tossed salad, and brownies

Vegetarian Alternative: Spaghetti, ziti, pasta salad

Beverages: Unlimited beer, wine, soft drinks, coffee, and tea

Description & Comments   The audience, attending a celebration for mobster Al Capone at a '30s speakeasy in Chicago, enters through a secret door using a password. The show is a musical of sorts, with most songs from other sources sung by cast members to recorded accompaniment. The story revolves around Miss Jewel—the speakeasy's hostess, who loves Detective Marvel, the only cop in Chicago that Capone can't buy—and one of the show's floozies and her gambling boyfriend. (Can you say, *Guys and Dolls?*)

The audience parades through the buffet line before the show; seconds are invited. The food is good for buffet fare. The lasagna is tasty, and it is nice to see variety on the line.

For a musical, this show employs a lot of nonsingers. Even the dancing is second-rate. The waiters—who speak with tough-guy accents and kid around with guests—did more to entertain the children than at any other show. Still, the theme is a bit too adult.

Wild Bill's Wild West Dinner Extravaganza

Address: 5260 US Highway 192, Kissimmee

Phone: (407) 351-5151

Show Times: Vary; usually at 7 and 9:30 p.m. nightly

Reservations: Need to make reservations a day or two in advance

Cost: $37; $23 ages 3–11 (does not include tax or tip)

Discounts: Florida residents, AAA, military, AARP; coupons in most tourist publications

Type of Seating: Long tables surround a stage where acts are performed in-the-round. The room has the look of a mess hall at an Old West fort.

Menu: Stew, salad, fried chicken, vegetables, baked potato, corn, baked beans, and ice cream cake

Vegetarian Alternative: Cheese ravoili or seasonal fish with advance request

Beverages: Unlimited beer, wine, and soft drinks

Description & Comments It's 1876 and Wild Bill and his co-host, Miss Kitty, are celebrating America's centennial with a show right out of the Wild West. Featured are knife throwers, archery demonstrations, rope tricks, saloon-hall dancers, and Native Americans.

Wild Bill's is a lot of fun, and the acts are first-rate. The Native American who performs a traditional hoop dance is fascinating. The room is divided, with half of the audience ranchers (lots of mooing) and the other half sheepherders (lots of baaing). There's plenty to keep the kids entertained. Whoever sits at the front of the table has the dubious task of serving much of the food to others at the table.

King Henry's Feast

Address: 8984 International Drive, Orlando

Phone: (407) 351-5151

Show Times: Vary; usually two shows nightly at 7 and 9:30 p.m.

Cost: $37; $23.99 ages 3–11

Reservations: Need to make reservations a day or two in advance

Discounts: Florida residents, AAA, military, AARP; coupons in most tourist publications

Type of Seating: Long tables encircle a stage where acts perform in-the-round.

Menu: Leek and potato soup, salad, fried chicken, barbecue pork, baked potato, corn on the cob, vegetables, cake, and ice cream

Vegetarian Alternative: Cheese ravioli or white fish entree with advance request

Beverages: Unlimited beer, wine, and soft drinks

Description & Comments It's King Henry's birthday, and the celebration in his summer castle includes a show that would have made Ed Sullivan proud. The monarch and his jester are hosts, introducing such acts as a trapeze aerialist, a juggler, and a sword swallower who will make your throat throb. There's also lots of singing and a lame sword fight.

Most acts are impressive, but the main characters—the king, his jester, and a woman who helps them sing the food into the hall—seem bored and they more or less walk through the evening.

The food is neither bad nor good. Each course, or "remove" as it's called, is paraded in by serving wenches, who plop the containers onto the table for the poor dope sitting on the end to dish up and pass down the way.

Kids will find the acts entertaining, but they may get bored with the traditional English folk songs, even when the audience is encouraged to sing along.

Pirates at Colossal Studios

Address: 6400 Carrier Drive, Orlando

Phone: (407) 248-0590

Show Times: 7:45 p.m. daily

Cost: $38; $23 ages 3–11 (does not include tax or tip)

Reservations: Can be made up to the day of the show

Discounts: Florida residents, AAA, AARP, military

Type of Seating: Arena-style

Menu: Caribbean rice with pineapple, pork, beef with mushroom gravy, and roasted chicken; fresh vegetables; ice cream and apple cobbler

Vegetarian Alternative: Lasagna

Beverages: Unlimited beer, wine, and soft drinks

Description & Comments   Setting is an old B-movie studio that used to make adventure movies. The audience sits in a lounge to watch a rehearsal for a new movie about pirates. Barrels fall off the wall, revealing the entrance to an old movie set. This is the dining area, centered by a life-size pirate ship surrounded by water. The crew begins filming on the newly discovered set.

The set is impressive, and during the evening pirates swoop from overhead, race around the ship on water scooters, toss balls into a net with the help of audience volunteers, and bounce on a trampoline that's part of the ship. What's mystifying is that there doesn't seem to be a reason for any of this. My companion and I were completely lost as to what was going on and why.

Audience members sit in color-coded sections and are encouraged to cheer for pirates wearing their colors as they compete against each other.

There's plenty to interest kids. Adults might be interested, too, if the story were easier to follow. After the show, guests are invited into a disco for dancing.

Aloha! Polynesian Luau

Address: Sea World, 7007 Sea World Drive, Orlando

Phone: (407) 351-3600

Show Times: 6:15 p.m. nightly

Reservations: Need to make reservations at least three days in advance

Cost: $36; $26 ages 8–12, $16 ages 3–7

Discounts: Discounts seasonally

Type of Seating: Long tables; no separation from other parties

Menu: Fruit "pu pu" platter, salad, mahimahi in piña colada sauce, sweet-and-sour chicken, smoked pork loin, rice, vegetables, and hula pie (cheesecake)

Vegetarian Alternative: Mixed vegetables, sticky rice

Beverages: One complimentary mai tai; full cash bar. This is the only show to offer just one cocktail, an odd thing considering the park is owned by Anheuser-Busch, which owns practically all the beer in the world.

Description & Comments *Aloha! Polynesian Luau* has the appearance of a touring lounge act that might play the Ramada Inn circuit in the Midwest. Even the venue, a large, dark room with a very low ceiling, looks like a motel lounge. In this musical revue featuring singers, dancers, and fire twirlers, a Don Ho–esque singer is given way too much time. The dancers perform well, and the fire twirler who ends the show is impressive, but there is otherwise little excitement.

The food is more varied than at many shows. The mahimahi is good, but the fruit platter is uninteresting. The food is served family-style, and you may share a platter with someone else's family.

The service is not very attentive. Audience participation is minimal, and children probably will be bored.

Sleuths Mystery Show

Address: Republic Square, 7508 Republic Drive, Orlando

Phone: (407) 363-1985

Show Times: Vary nightly; 6, 7:30, or 9 p.m.

Cost: $36.95; $22.95 ages 3–11 (does not include tax or tip)

Reservations: Can be made up to the day of the show

Discounts: Coupon for Florida residents, AAA, seniors, students, Disney employees, travel agents, military, hospitality employees, full-blooded Chippewa Indians

Type of Seating: Large round tables that seat 8–10; some smaller tables

Menu: Cheese spread and crackers; tossed salad; choice of Cornish hen, prime rib (at an extra $3 charge), or lasagna; veggies and a baked potato; mystery dessert

Vegetarian Alternative: Cheese lasagna

Beverages: Unlimited beer, wine, or soft drinks

Description & Comments   Sleuths perform a repertory of murder mysteries the audience must solve. Audience participation is key to the enjoyment. Guests are part of the show from the moment they enter the theater. Actors in character direct seating and try to drop clues as to who and what their parts are in the play. Although they work from a script, much of the show is ad-libbed. Unfortunately, the cast tends to be of limited talent and incapable of ad-libbing well. Each table must choose a spokesman and prepare a question for the actors as they try to solve the murder. Unless you come with a large group, you probably will find yourself interacting with strangers.

The cheese spread and crackers—one crock and one basket for the entire table—is about as cheesy an appetizer as you'll find. The salad is a bigger joke than any the actors produce. The prime rib was tough during our visit, and the Cornish hen had little meat.

You'll probably have more fun if you go with a large group and occupy your own table. Older children might find the show inter-esting, but younger ones will probably be bored.

Church Street Station

Before there was Pleasure Island, Downtown Disney, or Universal Studios CityWalk, there was Church Street Station, a place for those in search of Orlando nightlife. Church Street Station is a group of several vintage buildings from the 1880s that were renovated in the 1970s. It features the most beautiful venues in downtown Orlando, complete with wide-open spaces, balconies, sparkling chandeliers, and pressed-tin ceilings.

If you're planning a family vacation, a stop at Church Street Station may be worth the price of admission, which is $17.95 plus tax for adults and $11.95 for children ages 4–12. Kids and adults really do have fun here, and the atmosphere is far removed from the "see and be seen" crowd at other downtown establishments. For this fee, which is charged only in the evening, you'll have access to Rosie O'Grady's, The Cheyenne Saloon, and The Orchid Garden. All offer live music and entertainment, welcoming young and old alike. Each venue performs three different sets every weeknight, and four sets each night on the weekends. The times are spaced so you can wander from venue to venue without missing a beat. There also are many areas that you can enjoy free, including the shops in Church Street Exchange, the Church Street Arcade, and the performers that mill around the street.

For those over age 21 and traveling without kids, consider what most locals know—there's more to this street than its formal Church Street Station venues. After bypassing the high-price ticket booth and crossing the railroad tracks, you'll find many bars and clubs that have little or no cover charge. There also is a vast array of restaurants offering almost anything your heart desires, from pizza and wings to sushi, all at moderate prices.

Wondering why you'd drive downtown when your hotel is just minutes away from Pleasure Island or CityWalk? The biggest difference between the theme park giants' entertainment areas and Church Street Station is that Church Street has more of a local, feel. If you like the feel of a true downtown area and you're ready for a break from Fantasyland, downtown Orlando is where it's at.

If visiting an authentic, local attraction isn't a priority and you are simply trying to choose between the three nighttime venues, it depends on what kind of experience you're looking for. Those seeking family fun should be aware that Disney's Pleasure Island really is an adult scene. Though kids may be welcome with an adult, Pleasure Island only offers bar hopping and a few sidewalk dance performances. In contrast, Church Street Station provides great entertainment for all ages for roughly the same ticket price (depending on whether you've purchased a Park Hopper Plus pass at Disney). But consider this: The entire Downtown Disney entertainment district (excluding Pleasure Island) provides many family options, including themed restaurants, kid-friendly shops like the Lego Imagination Center, and DisneyQuest, an interactive arcade. True, you can also visit this area during the day, but it takes on a more festive feel after sunset.

If you're looking for nightlife sans the kids, you may have a difficult decision. All three locations offer the requisite bars and nightclubs. Also, each features many choices for live music. Some might appreciate CityWalk because, unlike Pleasure Island, you can visit each bar individually. This allows you to choose your experience without forking over the hefty admission fee. However, you can also do this at Church Street if you avoid the formal venues at Church Street Station and hit the pubs and bars like Mulvaney's and One Eyed Jack's.

Something else to consider: If you like to dance, Pleasure Island is tops, with five clubs that cover all bases. Dancing at CityWalk is more varied, from the band at Bob Marley's to the spicy sounds of The Latin Quarter, but they do not necessarily appeal to all groups. Dancing at Church Street takes more effort, as only a few of the clubs offer this diversion.

GETTING THERE

Church Street Station is located in the heart of downtown Orlando. From Disney and the International Drive area, take Interstate 4 east to Anderson Street (exit 38). Follow the signs to Boone Avenue. From there, either head straight into the parking lot that charges a flat fee of $5, or if you're only staying a few hours, turn left on South Street, then make an immediate right on Garland Avenue. On the left, under the I-4 overpass, is a city parking lot that charges by the hour. Valet parking is available at Church Street and Garland Avenue.

Touring Tips If you're frightened about your safety while visiting downtown Orlando, there's really no need to worry. Just remain alert and cautious as you would in any unfamiliar location. All of the parking options are safe, but young women traveling alone might feel more secure in the well-lit garage as opposed to the open-air city lot under I-4. Often, Orlando police officers and security guards can be found in both locations. In the city lot, they are usually doling out parking tickets to folks whose meters have expired, so keep this in mind as well.

ADMISSION PRICES

Following are the ticket prices for the formal Church Street Station venues (includes admission to Rosie O'Grady's, The Cheyenne Saloon, The Orchid Garden, and all live shows):

Adults: $17.95 + tax
Children (ages 4–12): $11.95

ARRIVING

Church Street Station—including the arcade, shops, and restaurants—is open from 11 a.m. to 2 a.m., and live shows (that require the admission fee) begin around 7:30 p.m. Discounted tickets are available for seniors with AARP membership cards, and often there is a Florida resident discount. Tickets can be purchased at the box office on Church Street. While you're there, grab a brochure that lists performance times.

The nice thing about Church Street Station shows is that you don't have to follow the clock of a college student. Nightlife begins long before 11 p.m., with shows starting early enough that you and your family can have some fun and get a good night's sleep. (This does not hold true at the bars and clubs outside of Church Street Station along Church Street, which begin to heat up around 9 p.m.) Weekends are busier than weekdays, but the three paid venues have plenty of seats, so chances are you won't have to stand.

CONTACTING CHURCH STREET STATION

For more information, call (407) 422-2434 or visit the Web site at www.churchstreetstation.com, which also lists any seasonal discounts.

Church Street Station's Clubs

Rosie O'Grady's

What It Is: Dixieland jazz hall

Cuisine: Sandwiches and snacks

Entertainment: Shows are at 7:15 p.m., 8:40 p.m., and 9:55 p.m.

Comments This Dixieland band, clad in red bow-ties and suspenders, will take you back in time. Performers strum bangos, bang on washboards, and belt out songs such as *Yankee Doodle Dandy.* Later in the set, a burlesque singer by the name of Red Hot Mama coaxes older men out of the audience for duets and dance numbers. This is crowd participation at its embarrassing best. If Red Hot Mama doesn't get your attention, the cancan girls surely will as they slide down a firehouse pole to perform their kicks and splits. Rosie's also offers edibles with a basic menu of snack food, including deli sandwiches, hot dogs, and popcorn.

Seating is available on the lower level and the balcony. Be sure to sit on the opposite side of the bar if you want to see the cancan girls—they climb onto the bar during a dance number.

Orchid Garden

What It Is: Rock-and-roll den, featuring music mainly from the 1950s and '60s

Cuisine: Only popcorn served

Entertainment: Shows are at 8 p.m., 9:20 p.m., and 10:40 p.m. weeknights; an 11:50 p.m. show is added Friday and Saturday

Comments Although very talented, this group of performers seemed very unenthusiastic, lacking the spontaneity and energy found in the other shows. True oldies fans will surely love it, though. If you're one of them, you'll find yourself singing along to popular ditties such as *Mack the Knife* and *Lollipop.* Even if you're not a fan of Bobby Darrin and the like, you'll love the beautiful old Orchid Garden venue. Unfortunately, Church Street Station has tried to theme this room by using props such as a juke box and a wax figure of Marilyn Monroe—completely tacky. But look beyond this facade and you'll see that the Orchid Garden itself is a real treasure. If you're looking to dance, this may be the place for you. There is only a small dance floor on the first level, but above the bandstand there is a circular dance floor that offers a larger space—if you don't mind being center stage.

Eat before you go—the Orchid Room only serves popcorn and drinks. Also, if a member of your group loves swing music, check out the Orchid Garden on Saturday nights. Free dance lessons are offered at 6:30 p.m., and the band begins at 8 p.m.

The Cheyenne Saloon and Opera House

What It Is: Country-music saloon

Cuisine: Barbecue

Entertainment: Shows are at 8:45 p.m., 10:10 p.m., and 11:25 p.m. on weeknights; a 12:45 a.m. show is added Friday and Saturday

Comments Grab a bar stool, partner. It's time to enjoy some honky-tonk music. Remember Kenny Rogers, Tanya Tucker, and Dolly Parton? Well, this country band remembers them, too, and knows that members of their audience may enjoy some of country music's finest recordings that radio stations seem to ignore. But don't think this band is stuck in a time warp. They can also cover country's most recent stars, such as Shania Twain.

The "lead singer" title is shared by three performers, one woman and two men, all equally talented performers. If you feel inspired, leave your seat at the horseshoe-shaped bar and head to the dance floor. If you'd rather just enjoy the music and the ambience, there are many seats in the multilevel saloon. The room features beautiful oak woodwork, antique pistol and rifle collections, and stuffed bear and moose heads hanging from the walls.

The Cheyenne Saloon is the only one of the three venues that offers a full-service restaurant. The Cheyenne Barbeque Restaurant serves beef, pork, chicken, and ribs. Most entrees are in the $13–15 range.

Phineas Phogg's

What It Is: Dance club, featuring music from the 1970s, '80s, and '90s

Cuisine: Free buffet on Fridays

Entertainment: Dancing to oldies played by a DJ

Special Comments: Must be age 21 or older to enter

Comments Expect to be surrounded by 20-somethings who just wanna have fun on a U-shaped dance floor. Brick walls, a long wooden bar, and wooden tables and stools provide ambience.

Locals used to drive from miles around for Nickel Beer Wednesday. Alas, the days of cheap beer in tiny plastic cups are over. Now, Friday Friends Happy Hour from 5:30 to 8:30 p.m. every Friday features bargain drinks and a free buffet.

Universal Florida CityWalk

CityWalk is a shopping, dining, and entertainment venue that doubles as the entrance plaza for the Universal Studios Florida and Islands of Adventure theme parks. Situated between the parking complex and the theme parks, CityWalk is heavily trafficked all day, but truly comes alive only at night.

In the evening CityWalk is Universal's answer to Disney's Pleasure Island and downtown Orlando's Church Street Station. Like its rivals, CityWalk offers a number of nightclubs to sample, but where Disney and Church Street tend to create their own clubs, CityWalk's entertainment and restaurant venues depend on well-known brand names. At CityWalk you'll find a Hard Rock Cafe and concert hall; Jimmy Buffet's Margaritaville; a Motown Cafe; NBA City, a sports bar; a NASCAR Cafe; and a branch of New Orleans' famous Pat O'Brien's club. City Jazz, a jazz club, works in cooperation with Downbeat Magazine, while a reggae club celebrates the life and music of Bob Marley. Only the Latin Quarter, a Latin American dance club and restaurant, and The Groove, a high-tech disco, operate without big-name tie-ins.

Another CityWalk distinction is that most of the clubs are also restaurants, or alternatively, most of the restaurants are also clubs. And although there's a lot of culinary variety, restaurants and nightclubs are different animals. Sight lines, room configuration, acoustics, intimacy, and atmosphere—important considerations in a nightclub—are not at all the same in a venue designed to serve meals. While it's nice to have all that good food available, the club experience is somewhat dulled. Working through the lineup, Pat O'Brien's, The Groove, and City Jazz are more nightclub than restaurant, while Margaritaville and the Motown Cafe are more restaurant than club. Bob Marley's and the Latin Quarter are half-and-half. The Hard Rock Live, NASCAR Cafe, NBA City, Emeril's, and Pastamore are restaurants.

Comparing CityWalk with its direct competitors, CityWalk offers more variety than Church Street Station but not as much as Disney's Pleasure Island (when combined with contiguous Disney's West Side). Noticeably absent at CityWalk are a comedy club and a country/western music venue. Parking at CityWalk is much easier than at Pleasure Island or Church Street, and dining at CityWalk is likewise superior to its rivals. Shopping at CityWalk is not as varied or interesting as at Downtown Disney, but is on a par with Church Street. Pleasure Island and CityWalk both offer outdoor stages, but not Church Street. You will find fewer under-21s at CityWalk than at Pleasure Island, but more than at Church Street.

In addition to the clubs and restaurants, there are (of course) shops and a Universal Cineplex multiscreen movie theater. In regard to the clubs, you can pay a cover in each one you visit or opt for a more expensive passport to all the clubs. Our advice is scope out the scene and pay as you go. Following are mini-profiles on each of the nightclubs.

GETTING THERE

The Universal Florida complex can be accessed via Kirkman Road from I-4 exits 29B or 30A. Driving from the Walt Disney World area, exit I-4 onto Sandlake Road heading north (away from International Drive) and turn right onto Turkey Lake Road. Follow the signs to the Turkey Lake Road entrance.

ADMISSION PRICES

CityWalk has no inclusive admission fee, like Pleasure Island and Church Street Station. Each club sets its own admission price, and you pay as you go. We've included cover charges in each club's description to give an idea of what you can expect.

ARRIVING

Once within the Universal complex, you'll be directed to park in one of two multi-tiered parking garages. Parking runs about $6 for cars and $7 for RVs. Be sure to write down the location of your car before heading out of the garages—the evening will end on a considerably brighter note if you avoid wandering about the garages searching for the rental car. An alternative, if you're out for a special occasion or just want to have everything taken care of, Universal also offers valet parking for $12. From the garages, moving sidewalks transport you directly to CityWalk.

CONTACTING CITYWALK

Contact CityWalk through its parent, Universal Florida, at (800) 771-0080, or visit their website, www.universalstudios.com. Keep in mind, though, that parents don't always know quite what the children are up to, so your best bet may be to contact specific clubs directly when you reach the Orlando area.

CityWalk Clubs

Jimmy Buffet's Margaritaville

What It Is: Key West–themed restaurant and club

Operating Hours: 11 a.m.–2 a.m.

Cuisine: Caribbean, Florida fusion, and American

Entertainment: Live rock and island-style music after 10 p.m.

Cover: $3.25 after 10 p.m.

Comments   Jimmy's is a big place with three bars that turns into a nightclub after 10 p.m. If you eat dinner there, you'll probably want to find another vantage point when the band cranks up.

Bob Marley—A Tribute To Freedom

What It Is: Reggae restaurant and club

Operating Hours: 5 p.m.–1:30 p.m. Monday through Friday
   11 a.m.–1:30 a.m. Saturday and Sunday

Cuisine: Jamaican-influenced appetizers and main courses

Entertainment: Reggae bands in the outdoor gazebo after
   8 p.m.

Cover: $4.25 after 7 p.m. nightly

Comments   This club is a re-creation of Marley's home in Kingston, Jamaica, and contains a lot of interesting Marley memorabilia. The courtyard is the center of action.

Motown Cafe Orlando

What It Is: Motown-themed restaurant and club

Operating Hours: 5 p.m.–12 a.m. Sunday through Thursday
   5 p.m.–2 a.m. Friday and Saturday

Cuisine: American regional cuisine

Entertainment: Two groups that emulate the Temptations and
   the Supremes

Cover: $3.25

Comments Primarily a restaurant with entertainment on the
side. Live entertainment consists of short sets performed inter-
mittently throughout operating hours.

Latin Quarter

What It Is: Latin dance club and restaurant

Operating Hours: 11 a.m.–1:30 a.m.

Cuisine: Food from South and Central American nations.

Entertainment: Live Salsa, Merenque, and Latin Rock augmented by costumed dancers

Cover: $3.25 after 10 p.m.

Comments Ultra high energy club with some of the most interesting food and entertainment at CityWalk. On more temperate
nights check out the second floor verandah overlooking CityWalk.

The Groove

What It Is: High tech disco

Operating Hours: 9 p.m.–2 a.m.

Cuisine: No food

Entertainment: DJ plays club and dance tunes. Sometimes there
   are live bands.

Cover: $5.25

Comments Guests must be 21 or older to enter this tres chic club
designed to look like an old theater in the midst of restoration.
There are seven bars and several themed cubby holes for getting
away from the thundering sound system. Dancers are barraged with
strobes, lasers, and heaven knows what else. Wear your sunscreen.

Pat O'Brien's Orlando

What It Is: Dueling pianos sing-along club and restaurant

Operating Hours: 11 a.m.–1 a.m.

Cuisine: Cajun

Entertainment: Dueling pianos and sing-alongs

Cover: $3.25 after 6 p.m. for piano bar only

Comments A clone of the famous New Orleans club of the same name. You can dine in the courtyard or on the terrace without paying a cover. You must be age 21 or over for the piano bar or the main bar anytime, and for the courtyard after 8 p.m.

City Jazz

What It Is: Jazz club and themed restaurant

Operating Hours: 8:30 p.m.–1 a.m.

Cuisine: Tappas-style appetizers, light snacks, sushi, desserts

Entertainment: Live jazz

Cover: $5.25 after 8:30 p.m. Sometimes more depending on the talent.

Comments   Jazz club that's also home to Downbeat Magazine's Jazz Hall of Fame museum (open 3 p.m.–6 p.m.).

Hard Rock Live

What It Is: Live music concert hall and club

Operating Hours: 7 p.m.–???

Cuisine: Limited menu

Entertainment: House band performs weekdays with big-name groups taking over on weekends.

Cover: $9 for house band. Cover varies for name acts.

Comments   Great acoustics, comfortable seating, and good sight lines make this the best concert venue in town. House band is excellent. By the by, the Hard Rock Live concert hall and the Hard Rock Cafe restaurant are separate facilities.

Index

2000 Unofficial Guide **Reader Survey**

If you would like to express your opinion about central Florida's attractions or this guidebook, complete the following survey and mail it to:

> *Unofficial Guide* Reader Survey
> P.O. Box 43059
> Birmingham, AL 35243

Inclusive dates of your visit _____

Members of your party:	Person 1	Person 2	Person 3	Person 4	Person 5
Gender (M or F)	_____	_____	_____	_____	_____
Age	_____	_____	_____	_____	_____

How many times have you been to central Florida? _____

On your most recent trip, where did you stay? _____

Concerning accommodations, on a scale with 100 best and 0 worst, how would you rate:

The quality of your room? _____   The value for the money? _____
The quietness of your room? _____   Check-in/checkout efficiency? _____
Shuttle service to the parks? _____   Swimming pool facilities? _____

Did you rent a car? _____   From whom? _____

Concerning your rental car, on a scale with 100 best and 0 worst, how would you rate:

Pickup processing efficiency? _____   Return processing efficiency? _____
Condition of the car? _____   Cleanliness of the car? _____
Airport shuttle efficiency? _____

Concerning your touring:

Who in your party was most responsible for planning the itinerary? _____
What time did you normally get started in the morning? _____
Did you usually arrive at the theme parks prior to opening? _____
Did you return to your hotel for rest during the day? _____
What time did you normally go to bed at night? _____

On a scale with 100 best and 0 worst, rate your theme park experience:

Park	*Rating*	*Park*	*Rating*
Busch Gardens	_____	Universal Studios	_____
Cypress Gardens	_____	Universal Islands of	
Gatorland	_____	Adventure	_____
Kennedy Space Center	_____	Wet 'n Wild	_____
SeaWorld	_____	WaterMania	_____

Concerning your dining and nightlife experiences:

How many restaurant meals (including fast food) did you average per day? ____

How much (approximately) did your party spend on meals per day? ____

Favorite restaurant? _____

Favorite nightclub? _____

Did you buy this guide: Before leaving? ____ While on your trip? ____

How did you hear about this guide?

Loaned or recommended by a friend ____ Radio or TV ____

Newspaper or magazine ____ Bookstore salesperson ____

Just picked it out on my own ____ Library ____

Internet ____

What other guidebooks did you use on this trip? _____

_____

On the 100 best and 0 worst scale, how would you rate them? _____

_____

Using the same scale, how would you rate the *Unofficial Guide?* _____

Are *Unofficial Guides* readily available in bookstores in your area? _____

Have you used other *Unofficial Guides?* ____ Which one(s)? _____

Comments about your central Florida vacation or about the *Unofficial Guide:*

_____

_____

_____

_____

_____

_____

_____

_____

_____

_____